Learning at the Top

Titles available in the **McGraw-Hill Developing Organizations** Series

THE ORGANIZATIONAL LEARNING CYCLE
How We Can Learn Collectively
Nancy Dixon
ISBN 0–07707937–X

THE WISDOM OF STRATEGIC LEARNING
The Self Managed Learning Solution
Ian Cunningham
ISBN 0–07707894–2

DEVELOPING STRATEGIC THOUGHT
Rediscovering the Art of Direction Giving
Edited by Bob Garratt
ISBN 0–07707986–8

PERSONAL AND ORGANIZATIONAL TRANSFORMATION
The True Challenge of Continual Quality Improvement
Dalmar Fisher and William Torbert
ISBN 0–07707834–9

LEARNING COMPANIES IN PRACTICE
Michael Pearn, Chris Mulrooney and Keri Roderick
ISBN 0–07707744–X

A CONSULTANT'S JOURNEY
Roger Harrison
ISBN 0–07709089–6

THE COLLECTED PAPERS OF ROGER HARRISON
Roger Harrison
ISBN 0–07709090–X

For further information on these titles and other forthcoming books please contact

The Product Manager, Professional Books, McGraw-Hill Book Company Europe, Shoppenhangers Road, Maidenhead, Berkshire SL6 2QL, United Kingdom
Telephone ++(0) 1628 23432 Fax ++(0) 1628 770224

Learning at the Top

ALAN MUMFORD

McGraw-Hill Book Company

London · New York · St Louis · San Francisco · Auckland
Bogotá · Caracas · Lisbon · Madrid · Mexico
Milan · Montreal · New Delhi · Panama · Paris · San Juan
São Paulo · Singapore · Sydney · Tokyo · Toronto

Published by McGraw-Hill Book Company Europe
Shoppenhangers Road, Maidenhead, Berkshire, SL6 2QL, England
Telephone 01628 23432
Fax 01628 770224

British Library Cataloguing in Publication Data

Mumford, Alan
    Learning at the Top.—(McGraw-Hill
    Developing Organizations Series)
    I. Title   II. Series   658.312404

ISBN 0–07–709066–7

Library of Congress Cataloging-in-Publication Data

Mumford, Alan
    Learning at the top / Alan Mumford.
        p.   cm.
    Includes index.
    ISBN 0–07–709066–7
    1. Executives – Training of. 2. Communication in organizations.
3. Organizational change. I. Title
HD30.4.M85   1995   95–790
658.4'07124–dc20   CIP

12345   CUP   98765

Typeset by Computape (Pickering) Ltd., North Yorkshire
and printed and bound in Great Britain at the University Press, Cambridge

Printed on permanent paper in compliance with ISO Standard 9706

To Brian Barder, who encouraged me to do my first book review for a Cambridge journal and thereby put me on the literary path I followed 10 years later as described in Chapter 17.

To my wife Denise, who encouraged me to write my second book—a much more difficult commitment than the first.

Contents

Series preface

The McGraw-Hill *Developing Organizations* series is for people in the business of changing, developing and transforming their organizations. The books in the series bring together ideas and practice in the emerging field of organizational learning and development. Bridging theory and action, they contain new ideas, methods and models of how to get things done.

Organizational learning and development is the child of the organization development (OD) movement of the 1960s and 1970s. Then people like Schein, Beckhard, Bennis, Walton, Blake and Mouton defined a *change technology* which was exciting and revolutionary. Now the world has moved on.

The word 'technology' goes with the organization-as-machine metaphor. OD emphasized the *outside-in* application of 'behavioural science', which seems naïve in the context of the power-broking, influence and leverage of today's language. Our dominant metaphor of organizations as organisms or collective living beings requires a balancing *inside-out* focus of development and transformation of what is already there.

Learning is the key to our current dilemmas. We are not just talking about change. Learning starts with you and me, with the person—and spreads to others—if we can organize in ways which encourage it.

Learning is at a premium because we are not so much masters of change as beset by it. There is no single formula or image for the excellent company. Even the idea of 'progress' is problematic as companies stick to the knitting and go to the wall. Multiple possible futures, the need for discontinuity almost for the sake of it, means that we must be able to think imaginatively, to be able to develop ourselves and, in generative relationships with others, to continuously organize and reorganize ourselves.

Organizations are unique, with distinctive biographies, strengths and opportunities. Each creates its own future and finds its own development paths. The purpose of these books is not to offer ready-made tools, but to help you create your own tools from the best new ideas and practices around.

The authors in the series have been picked because they have something to say. You will find in all of the books the personal voice of the writer, and this reflects the voice which each of us needs in our own organizations to do the best we can.

Fellow members of the management development trade, Alan Mumford and I have travelled on similar roads, as part of the movement which has put learning at the heart of our business. In his book Alan deals with the issue of the learning of those most important people—those at the top of the organization. By 'most important' I don't mean to say that, as human beings, directors or senior managers are any more or less worthy of grace than the rest of us, but that in most of our companies they are the role models, the prime setters of the learning climate. However flat, participative or 'democratic' organizational structures become, those managers and directors are still likely to be the biggest single influence on how learningful their companies are.

When I asked Alan if he would share his wealth of experience gained from working with the concerns and preoccupations of top teams, I was pleased when he said yes, and then surprised and delighted at the speed and commitment with which he tackled the assignment.

In the tradition of this series, the voice here is personal—a new departure for the author, he tells us—and distinctive—sceptical, persistent, self-revelatory, tinged with a pawky humour. Alan's autobiographical essay (Chapter 17) goes even further than the idea that good books are always personal statements to illustrate how the person and the knowledge offered are part of the same whole. Welcome.

Mike Pedler

Introduction

This Introduction gives some of the reasons why this book has been written, and explains the tone of voice in which it is delivered, and describes the model of learning used.

What is a Learning Organization? I have read the proliferating articles and books on the learning organization with a mixture of pleasure, puzzlement and scepticism.

Pleasure, because the concept that an organization could both provide a context for, and be the active force in, a learning process provides great potential. The elevation of learning beyond the individual to the larger unit contains fascinating possibilities for effective interaction of individual, group and organizational action and learning. Perhaps even more importantly, it provides the possibility of placing learning on different agendas, and probably at higher levels, in many organizations than is often the case when learning is focused primarily on individual or even subgroup needs.

Puzzlement, because the concepts and constructs of organizational learning often seem elusive, sometimes seem contradictory with each other, and sometimes seem to claim purposes and achievements at a higher level than those dreamt of in my philosophy.

Scepticism may be the consequence of my now lengthy experience in management development, and of my awareness of the susceptibility of management development to flavours of the year and to my personal styles of thinking and learning, which emphasize analysis and reflection.

In combination, all these have made me wonder how appropriate some of the claims about organizational learning are. Is organizational learning a new discovery, given force, energy and persuasiveness by (particularly) Peter Senge and by Mike Pedler, John Burgoyne and Tom Boydell in the later 1980s? Or is it a rediscovery of themes and challenges first advanced by Chris Argyris 20 years earlier? Is it the innovative integration of ideas about learning in organizations? Is it, to use words particularly appropriate in this context, a re-framing of experiences which has led to a greater understanding of organizational learning? Or is it, sadly, not an innovation at all, not an integration, not a re-framing, but simply a re-naming?

My analytical and reflective cast of thought might seem naturally to take me into a sceptical mode. Yet my attitude to learning and development is primarily optimistic. My tendency is to see a glass of water as half full rather than half empty. When I was invited to write this book, I decided that it was an opportunity to review my experiences and assess in what sense if any they came near to helping to create a more effective learning organization.

Working with Directors

The series editor asked that I should give special emphasis to my work at the most senior levels in organizations—directors or their equivalents, similarly endowed with the status and power that could be of special significance for a learning organization. This was a particularly interesting proposition to me. Not only did I agree with the potential special contribution that top people in organizations might have made, but I believed that the most demanding and highest potential features of a learning organization cannot possibly be achieved unless people at the top have engaged in the values, principles and practices appropriate to a learning organization.

Individual learners can survive with relative effectiveness at any level and sometimes without serious organizational encouragement. It is arguable that the concepts of the learning organization will not be fully effective unless all individuals and all levels within an organization subscribe. I take the view that this is a desirable but not a necessary factor—desirable because everybody could and should make a contribution, from the apparently less important jobs right through to the chief executive. However, it is a ludicrous form of egalitarianism to suppose that the contribution of a storeroom clerk is as vital to the learning organization as that of a director on the board. The contribution of people at the top is crucial, because it is there that the nature, purposes and culture of the organization are decided, whatever the arrangements may have been for communication, consultation and perhaps even consensus about such issues.

In making these observations about the significance of

organizational learning being both modelled on and driven by people at the top, the personal experiences reviewed in this book coincide with an awareness of history within management and organizational development. One of the reasons why the Organization Development Movement largely faded away after the 1970s' enthusiasm for it was that all too often it was introduced by advisers and consultants who either did not have access to the top or were unable to persuade the top people in organizations to take the notions of organization development aboard. Since a number of the inherent values proposed for organizational learning, especially by Mike Pedler and his colleagues, are similar to those of the Organization Development Movement (values such as openness, trust, sharing and positive use of conflict), it is important that we do not repeat past errors in the enthusiasm for a new process, especially when it contains so much of the vocabulary of the old.

Tone and Style

This book is much more personal in tone and content than anything else I have written. The reasons for this are interrelated but not complex. My normal style in dealing with managers one to one or in small workshops is characteristically analytical, reflective, controlled, emotionally cool. Generally, I seek to cause people to think more carefully than they probably otherwise would do about their experiences, about their work, about their interrelationships; I do not feel it appropriate that my intervention should be very obtrusive. My books generally reflect this aspect of my behaviour—they are descriptive and analytical, but include exercises designed to cause readers to think more for themselves.

In larger groups, particularly of the vastly mixed nature encountered at conferences, other aspects of my style come forward. Feedback from such conferences is often complimentary in terms of clarity of exposition and relative novelty of thought. Conference participants who have previously read my articles and books are particularly likely to notice that I introduce additional elements. My conference performances are much more obviously personal in the sense that I am seen to perform with enthusiasm (indeed, sometimes with passion) and that my deployment of irony as a technique does not in the end conceal how strongly I feel about some of the issues on which I speak.

My previous books have attempted to give helpful answers to the practical problems of management development. They reflect the objectives I had in writing them; they are well ordered and present the results of years of experience in management development. They do not, however, fully reveal the nature of my experience. They smooth away some of the jagged realities of experience in the quite legitimate pursuit of facilitating understanding and action by the reader.

In this book I have chosen to use a different voice. Learning through action has been, both for myself and for those who have participated in the process with me, much less planned, organized, coherent and neat than I might have liked it to have been. One of the major arguments in this book is that task and learning are inextricably interwoven. The greater the extent to which the mutuality of the two is recognized, the closer we get to organizational learning. But we know, from managerial research and from our own experience, how messy, disorganized and relatively incoherent a great deal of managerial action is. In this book I have attempted to write not with the Olympian detachment of 'one of the UK's leading management development experts' (chairman's description before a conference speech), but with the engaged, sometimes angry, sometimes confused, sometimes amused style more representative of what I was actually going through at the time.

I do not pretend that this means that everything here meets Oliver Cromwell's injunction about a portrait that it should be 'warts and all'. The more personal the story, the more likely the unconscious pressure for self-justification. As Oscar Wilde said, 'The truth is never pure and rarely simple.'

The cases I quote are incomplete in another sense. Some of my experiences would have no legitimacy in terms of helping others to operate in this field, however fascinating they may be in terms of self-analysis or perhaps even to others in terms of a gossip-level interest. The point of sharing experiences in this book is not just that they should be interesting, but that they should have transferable meaning to others. Many managerial autobiographies seem not to believe in the necessity of this conjunction, although their sales may not have been badly damaged as a result.

It was said of Winston Churchill that he wrote a book supposedly about the First World War, actually about himself, and called it 'The World Crisis'. I hope this book, intended as an honest learning review of a consultant's casebook, does not appear to be a love letter to myself. I have explained the relatively personal flavour of the book. However, it is one thing to paint the warts on my own face (Cromwell asked that his portraitist should put them in); but none of the organizations whose experiences I have used in this book asked me to write about *them*, with or without warts.

It would be interesting and would also add meaning if I had quoted the names of the organizations with which I have been involved, if not of the individuals themselves. I have written several articles naming organizations, in each case only after I have gone to them and sought permission for the detailed contents of the article. Here, however, I wanted to say things that such organizations would not necessarily welcome, so all the detail is delivered anonymously. It was more feasible to adopt an absolute rule of anonymity than to quote some organizations, or aspects of particular work with some organizations, openly. Confidentiality is a crucial aspect of the kind of work described here. To a considerable extent, the book represents my attempt to find a comfortable position between a rock (desire to communicate) and a hard place (confidentiality). Individuals who think they recognize themselves in the book may be pleased or annoyed—and they may be right or wrong. They may all congratulate themselves on having aided the cause of more effective learning.

I once had to carry out an appraisal with someone who had to respond to the question, 'What areas for improvement do you think to be necessary in your own performance?' He said to me in absolute seriousness that he had thought about this question for a long time and 'I really cannot identify any.' I love and have learned from my successes; I am upset by and learn from my mistakes. I have included self-criticism at various points, and two major cases in Chapter 15. In order to ensure that I do not conceal mistakes from which others might learn, I have included a specific chapter about myself (Chapter 17).

Keeping a Memory

On the Honey–Mumford Learning Styles Descriptions, I am a Strong Reflector. I keep notes on discussions I have with clients, and when I run programmes I make detailed notes of what has occurred. I also keep a notebook in which I review significant events and occurrences. In so far as I am wiser after the event, it is in part because I keep these reflective contemporaneous notes, which have increased the accuracy and reduced claims to undue wisdom during the event.

A Definition

Argyris, Senge, Pedler *et al.* have all offered their own powerful definitions of the learning organization. For a variety of reasons, I did not find any of the definitions congenial or helpfully usable with managers. Peter Honey and I combined to produce our own definition:

The learning organization is one that creates an environment where the behaviours and practices involved in continuous development are actively encouraged.
(Mumford, Alan. *Management Development: Strategies for Action*, IPM, 2nd Edition, 1993.)

The experiences reviewed in this book are tested against that definition. Whether they do or do not meet other people's definitions is for readers and other authors to decide.

Another Difference

The experiences, statements and conclusions offered here are not challenged or supported by a panoply of references to the work of other people. In my other books, references to the work of other people was obligatory and helpful. References here to the work of others occur when their work has been stirred into mine in some special sense, rather than where the work of others confirms or challenges what I have said.

What is Learning?

The book as a whole illustrates learning as:

• A process
• An achievement

In addition, it describes my learning as:

• A journey

The Content

The work described here consistently follows a pattern of moving from diagnosis to action. It seems logical to follow the same throughout the book. I have also followed the principles of the *learning cycle*, described below. So readers will find in each section, first, a description of an experience and reflections on that experience, followed by a statement of the conclusions I have drawn from having had the experience and reviewed it. In other books I have given much greater emphasis to the fourth stage of the learning cycle—i.e. planning the next steps. As a result the questions and exercises included at the ends of chapters in much of my other work, intended to aid readers in this process of 'planning', rather destroyed the personal tone. In this book, therefore, instead of including such exercises with each chapter or section, the following questions are offered for readers to employ if they choose and where they choose:

- How comparable have been any experiences I have had to those described here?
- What has been my review of my own experiences, and what do I think of the experiences described here?
- What conclusions can I draw from reviewing these two sets of experiences?
- What actions could I take as a result of these conclusions?

The Sequence

Some cases appear complete in one chapter; others appear in different chapters as particular stages or themes relevant to specific chapter topics. The cases are also broadly chronological. This has the virtue of showing the reality of the development of the ideas and processes described.

The work described in this book increasingly centres on the ideas and practices involved in implementing the learning cycle and recognizing individual preferences about learning—i.e. *learning styles*. The book itself follows the stages of the learning cycle. Instead of leaving a description of these in full to Part Two, which describes models, theories and diagnostic instruments, the learning cycle and learning styles are dealt with in this Introduction. Readers who are already familiar with the Honey–Mumford versions of these may prefer to move on and come back to the following descriptions later.

The Book as Model

The book exemplifies the proposition that the effective interaction of task and learning is one of the defining characteristics of the learning organization. It takes the variety of tasks with which I have been involved, and describes what I have learned from carrying them out. The general idea of the learning cycle, whether in the Lewin, Kolb, Revans or Honey–Mumford version has become increasingly well known over the last 15 years (Fig. I.1).

The book is illustrative also of one of the visual problems of the learning cycle, which can look as if it is an entirely enclosed model. In fact, Figs. I.2 and I.3 give useful additional concepts to the idea of learning and to how writing a book such as this exemplifies the process. In Fig. I.2 I attempt to show that any particular learning experience can involve revisiting some part of the cycle—engaging in more reflection, or recognizing that you have not reached sufficiently clear conclusions. In Fig. I.3 I use the idea of the *learning spiral* (separately developed by Professor John Morris and Peter Honey), which projects the idea of learning being a

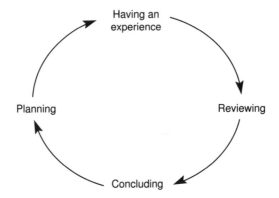

Fig. I.1   The learning cycle
Source: P. Honey and A. Mumford, *Manual of Learning Styles*, 3rd ed, Honey, 1992

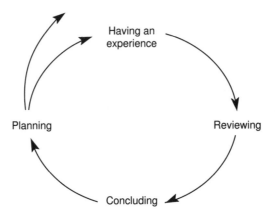

Fig. I.2   The progressive learning cycle
Source: A. Mumford, *How Managers Can Develop Managers*, Gower, 1993

continuous process in which one experience is taken forward and built on.

The Learning Process

Readers will better understand the structure of the book, and the material in the early chapters, after reading the following explanation of the learning cycle and learning styles.

There is a symbiotic relationship between the task cycle and the learning cycle. To use the words I would employ if I were not sure of the intellectual level of my audience, they are mutually consistent and interdependent.

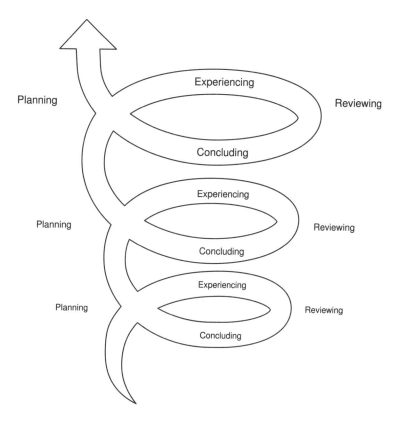

Fig. I.3 The learning spiral: learning as a continuous process
Source: P. Honey and A. Mumford, *Manual of Learning Styles*, 3rd ed,
Honey, 1992

The fact that managers and organizations are not required
to make an immense leap in their thinking processes from task
to learning is fundamental to the chances of obtaining
commitment to the idea of learning effectively through task.
(see Fig. I.4).

However, the fact that the thinking processes are so very
similar could be a seductive but inappropriate conclusion, if
managers therefore felt they need not give explicit attention to
the learning process. In fact, they do need to, because,
whereas consciously or unconsciously the sequence of the task
cycle *is* familiar to them, that of the learning cycle is most
unlikely to be familiar as a disciplined, articulate process—
though it may form a part of their often unconscious,
inarticulated experience.

If the learning organization is to be effective, it must be built
on an explicit understanding of how effective learning is
achieved. That means time must be given to explain to

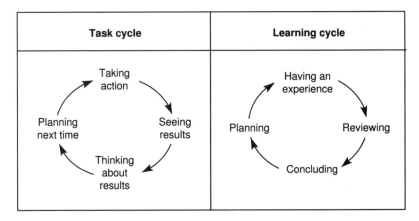

Fig. I.4   The task cycle and the learning cycle
Source: P. Honey and A. Mumford, *Manual of Learning Opportunities*,
Honey, 1989

managers what the learning process is and how they can use
it more effectively, both as individuals and as a group.

The four stages of the learning cycle can be illustrated as
follows.

1. *Having an experience*: Tim attended the first meeting held by
   a new managing director.
2. *Reviewing the experience*: After the meeting he compared
   notes with his colleagues on the way in which their new
   boss had chaired the meeting. They all agreed that the
   meeting had been both more purposeful and more involving than meetings run by his predecessor.
3. *Concluding from the experience*: Tim decided that there were
   a number of aspects of the way in which his new boss
   chaired the meeting that led him and others to feel happier
   and more energized as a result. He thought there were a
   number of ideas about running meetings which he could
   use.
4. *Planning the next steps*: Tim decided to plan a meeting with
   his own managers, using some of the ideas he had
   identified. In addition, however, he decided that he would
   start the meeting by stating a number of the changes he
   was making, rather than just making them.

In the above example, Tim was not at the time conscious of
learning—he just thought he had been through a process
called 'picking up and using good ideas'. It was only when he
was asked to think about useful experiences that he had had,

in one of my research projects, that he recognized that this was 'learning'.

Still at an individual level, the following example is taken from an activity that is explicitly about learning, rather than drawn from work.

1. *Having an experience*: John, who had been a functional director in a large manufacturing company for six years, agreed to go on an outdoor management training course. The course was full of the familiar outdoor activities—bridging ravines, finding locations at night, etc.
2. *Reviewing the experience*: 'This kind of course is often described as being about leadership. It wasn't that for me. I really understood for the first time what an effective team could be like.'
3. *Concluding from the experience*: 'I think I have been misled, or have fooled myself, about the extent to which I was really working with a team in my own division. I was also wrong about what leadership really means. I really did think it was getting people to do what you wanted them to do. I realized through this course that it is much more about a team deciding what needs to be done and then working together to ensure that it happens.'
4. *Planning the next steps*: John set out in his mind how he would explain to the people he had previously called subordinates, but now saw more as his fellow team members, what he had learned from the course and what he proposed they do about it.

Individual Learning Styles

The inherent logic of the learning cycle is readily accepted by managers and directors. If, as I always try to do, the explanation is presented in association with the task cycle, the level of belief is even higher. Some of them will want to discuss whether you always enter at the 'having an experience' stage. The basic elements, however, are always accepted by practising managers and directors, though academics sometimes find a four-stage process much too simple.

It would be marvellous if all individuals were complete all-rounders in the sense of equal commitment, involvement and ability at each of the four stages. They are not. Directors are aware—though imperfectly so, until it is discussed with them—that individuals vary in their interest or capacity to learn from all four stages of the cycle. Their recognition of this can be drawn out from discussion—for example, by asking participants on a programme, or individuals working on personal development plans, what their own learning experiences have been, and then establishing correlations with preferences about stages of the cycle.

Alternatively, and depending on the occasion, I present the argument for learning styles with all my authority as 'one of the UK's leading experts in learning processes'. It is better to develop the case, but time does not always allow it. So I usually move from a description of the learning cycle and the four stages to the proposition that, not only do individuals vary in their interest in and ability on the four stages, but it is possible to identify which individuals prefer which stage of learning through the Honey–Mumford Learning Styles Questionnaire. The association between the four stages and the four learning styles is demonstrated through Fig. I.5.

The full details of the Learning Styles Questionnaire—its construction, validity, reliability and all the other important questions about its nature—are spelled out in the *Manual of Learning Styles* (Peter Honey and Alan Mumford, 1992). For present purposes it is necessary only to summarize the four learning styles, as follows.

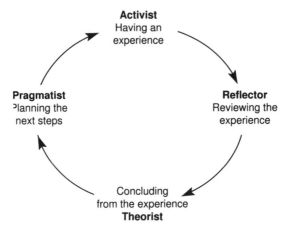

Fig. I.5   Learning styles and the learning cycle
Source: P. Honey and A. Mumford, *Manual of Learning Styles*, 3rd ed, Honey, 1989

Activists

- Activists enjoy the here-and-now and are happy to be dominated by immediate experiences.
- Their philosophy is 'I'll try anything once.
- They tend to act first and consider the consequences afterwards.

- They thrive on the challenge of new experiences, but are relatively bored with implementation and longer-term consolidation.

Reflectors

- Reflectors collect data, both first-hand and from others, and prefer to think about it thoroughly before coming to any conclusion.
- They like to consider all possible angles and implications before making a move.
- They often come over as relatively cautious and may have a low profile.
- They like to stand back to think about experiences and observe them from many different perspectives.

Theorists

- Theorists are keen on basic assumptions, principles, theories, models and systems.
- They prize rationality and logic.
- They tend to be detached and analytical.
- They like to assemble disparate facts into coherent theories.
- They prefer logic to lateral thinking or subjective judgements.

Pragmatists

- Pragmatists are very interested in new ideas provided they are relevant to their current context.
- They tend to look for new ideas and things with which to experiment—again, provided they appear to be relevant.
- They may tend to be impatient with ruminating and open-ended discussion.

The above are very much shortened elements of the general descriptions we have developed for these learning styles. They were explicitly designed to be about recognizable managerial behaviour, rather than about specifically 'learning' behaviour. (Honey and I thought the sensible starting-point was the *general* behaviour in which learning is grounded, rather than trying to identify, as does David Kolb, *learning* behaviour, which in fact managers have rarely thought about.) The general descriptions provide the initial validation for individuals who have secured their learning styles scores. 'Is that really like me—am I that strong in my preference, or that low?' Beyond the general descriptions is a set of statements we produced which suggest the activities a manager will learn best from and those he or she will learn least well from.

The Learning Cycle and Learning Styles: Argument and Illustration

This book describes what I have done. It does not include discussion about the derivation of the learning cycle (Lewin, Kolb, Revans) or about my indebtedness to David Kolb for his unique innovation of identifying learning styles. My experience is that discussion of the learning process and of individual learning styles is liberating, not restricting. People stay in a constricted box—'I am a Strong Reflector'—only if that is what they want to do or are allowed to do.

One application of learning styles will be shown in Chapter 5, where the significance of individual learning styles for personal development plans is illustrated. Chapter 12 provides an even more substantial case, involving the use of the learning cycle and learning styles for two purposes: the production of personal development plans, and the design of the director development programme as a whole.

I cannot remember a session with managers and directors in which the learning cycle and learning styles has not generated interest and fascination among participants. Kurt Lewin said 'there is nothing so practical as a good theory'. This statement suits three strong learning preferences—Reflector, Theorist and Pragmatist. I always emphasize the word 'good' in Lewin's statement; then I move on to the word 'practical'. This is because, however interested and fascinated managers may have been, the purpose is far more ambitious than to run an interesting session which would get good marks on an end-of-course happiness sheet: clients should be enabled to do something with the information I am giving them.

The feedback on later application is less dramatically satisfying. My clients recognize and use these ideas while on my workshops, but there is less evidence about how much they use it afterwards. (See my weakness discussed in Chapter 6.) I have to rely on particular anecdotes from individuals I may meet in subsequent activities. There such anecdoted reports show that the process is worth while—but it is the area in which I feel that the absolute assurance of my optimism could be challenged.

The fact is, I *believe*; and I know that I convey that belief with such certainty and conviction that my clients are drawn along with me. My belief is joined by their recognition of a sensible interpretation of their own experience. I am sustained by an intellectual conviction of the logic of the descriptions, by many warming experiences of my own with individuals (and now of a large number of trainers and developers with their own clients), and by an absolute certainty that what I am providing is not an interesting titbit such as a personality test, but something that is the key to effective learning.

Organizations sometimes talk about and write about core values—this is one of mine.

Readers with Learning Style Preferences

Of course, readers may have strong preferences. So pragmatists and activists will be interested particularly in answers—especially Chapters 5, 12 and 13; reflectors will like the diagnostic and research chapters—1, 2, 3 and 9; theorists may particularly value Chapters 7, 10, 11 and 14. I hope, however, that all my readers will be flexible enough to learn something from all the chapters.

PART ONE

DO YOU THINK YOU COULD HELP US?

Some Explanation of Part One

The chapters in this Part follow the sequence of my involvement with directors and senior managers. However, readers will better understand the content of each of these stages if they know more about the values, beliefs and practices that have directed my approach.

Where Are You Coming From?

A little boy once asked his mother, 'Where did I come from?' His mother had prepared herself for this day and went carefully over the loving process involved in sexual reproduction, aided by a modern book with illustrative pictures. The young boy listened enthralled. 'Actually what I meant was Johnny says his family came from Birmingham and I wondered where we came from.'

The locational answer to the question is that, in all but two of the cases mentioned in this Part, I was an external consultant. For nine years I was operating from International Management Centres, an innovative independent business school based on the philosophy of action learning. For the last four years I have been an independent consultant.

In many ways, the more significant issue is where I come from in terms of the philosophy and detailed practices I offer. The following paragraphs attempt to summarize these issues:

1. Effective learning occurs most frequently from work on real issues, problems, opportunities. This is the prime driving force for my work. Projects and tasks are not an interesting supplement to development programmes, but a primary purpose. Development programmes built on this philosophy provide double value—achieved real work, and learning.

2. Learning has to be explained and directed as an explicit managerial process. The strength of learning through

action can lead to the perennial problem of managers being seduced into frenetic activity. The good news is that, as shown in the Introduction, the thinking processes involved in managerial tasks and managerial learning are essentially the same.

3. Learning is an individual process which occurs most of the time for directors and managers within a social, i.e. group, context. However, it is personal not only in terms of what individuals choose to learn in terms of content, but in terms of how they like to learn. The good news is that the marvellous variation in human beings is reflected in which form of learning they prefer just as it is in which hobbies they pursue and what sort of holidays they like. The bad news is that this individuality provides obstacles for any learning experience offered to individuals or groups, who may have stronger or weaker desires to learn from particular kinds of experience (different learning styles).

4. Three things combine to make me suspicious of, and reluctant to offer, standard solutions along the lines of 'all directors need to be able to ...'. First, most of the management research in the United States and the United Kingdom over the last 20 years has illustrated time and again that the reality of managerial work is contingent upon the nature and purposes of the organization in which the manager works. This finding is desperately inconvenient for those who want to establish a supposedly professional managerial qualification in the United Kingdom, and therefore it has largely been ignored.

   A second feature is that standard solutions are a convenience. They seems to offer a relatively economical 'solution' to apparently recognized problems. Apart from the issue of whether an inappropriate answer can in any sense be 'economical', the probability is that the profit lies with the provider rather than with the receiver.

   The third issue is that standardized solutions not only tend to ignore the specific reality of particular organizations in terms of 'needs', but, as suggested immediately above, they do not sufficiently recognize and deal with the issues of individual learning preferences. While this is most obviously true on the issue of individual development plans (see Chapters 3 and 4), it is also true for group learning programmes.

As will be seen in Chapter 1, my work always starts by helping the organization define what the issues and problems are. The diagnostic phase is not simply a precursor to a development programme, but sometimes is a stand-alone process. Of course, it is more expensive at first sight to undertake careful analysis than it is to offer a standard programme. The case for it has to be made explicit in early discussion with the client. Most of the organizations described in this book did not, at the time of initial contact, really know what problems they were trying to resolve. The idea that a more effective sequence of action could be designed following a careful discussion of real problems and issues was attractive to them.

It is also sensible to be explicit about the case for spending more money at the most senior level. If directors or their equivalents are not providing effective direction for the organization, the organization will not survive. It makes sense to invest relatively more money in work at senior levels. If trainers do not like the impact on their budgets, chief executives may insist that they and their colleagues get a larger share, or may provide the money directly from their own funds. I say to potential clients bluntly that more money should be spent at the top of the organization.

The Definition of Flexibility

A consequence of the overriding philosophy and practical approaches outlined above is that the work described in this book is custom-tailored. It is specific to particular organizations, groups and individuals. In addition to the content, the design process can be flexible as well. Five days? Five times one day? In Chapters 5 and 14 some of the issues involved in the design of programmes are discussed.

There are two constraints in the amount of flexibility I offer which are worth recognizing at this point. My starting proposition for any off-the-job process is that it must occur primarily on normal work-days. The programmes are designed around real work and therefore must not be seen or experienced as something that can be fitted in only at weekends. This is a crucial point in establishing the mind-set of those people making the decision about a programme and participants.

The second constraint was defined for me by one of my colleagues in the business school who had heard me many times describe how I design programmes with full careful diagnosis and with great flexibility in terms of content. 'Alan, compared with most of us you really are flexible. Except that the client has to accept that the programme will be built on the philosophy of action learning, and that they have to discuss their learning processes while they are on it.'

She was right—most particularly about the whole issue of

the explicit attention given to how individuals learn. The phrase 'learning to learn' is becoming one of the clichés of the management education and training world. Unless there is explicit discussion of what learning actually means, what the general process of learning for directors is and what the specific preferences of individuals are, I think the phrase is essentially meaningless in terms of real achievement on a programme. In too many cases, it has become a necessary sales insert in descriptive programme brochures, bearing no contact with what occurs on the programme.

Peter Senge has pointed out that 'individual learning does not guarantee organizational learning. But without it no organizational learning occurs.' (*The Fifth Discipline*, Doubleday, New York, 1990). Much organizational learning literature focuses too intensively on the need to change the nature of organizations, with very little attention being given to the practices and behaviours that actually would define a learning organization, as distinct from an organization suffused with high moral values and good managerial practices. Learning to learn is therefore a fundamental requirement for a learning organization. But we have business schools that would not dream of running programmes without explicit sessions on decision-making, negotiation, the environment, ethics—and yet never discuss learning!

It is a marginal judgement whether such schools are crazy, ignorant or inefficient in terms of their own objectives, which are often grandiose in terms of the claims made for what the programmes will achieve. In terms of their contribution to continued learning, which is surely a basic requirement for any programme run nowadays, and therefore in terms of their potential contribution to a learning organization, they have nothing to offer.

1   We Would Like to Talk to You About ...

The same case number applies to each organization throughout the book.

This chapter looks at diagnostic processes used where the main explicit issue was director effectiveness rather than development.

CASE 1

I was invited to meet three managers, two from personnel and one line, to discuss what they described as a 'management development problem'. The three managers provided a general statement of their perceptions of management style and of some of the issues in their unit, and then gave a more specific analysis of the 'problem' on which they wanted help. Their unit had carried out a major comparative study on the effectiveness of a competitor organization, and as a consequence had identified the need for changes. The major changes were to be both in the structure of the organization and in the style of managing.

At the time of our first meeting, not all the details of either structure or style had been decided, let alone implemented. However, one major point had been agreed upon in principle as a requirement for senior executives and managers throughout the international organization to which this unit belonged. As a consequence, in contrast with the previous management style, which these three managers described as hierarchic and authoritarian, the unit director and his fellow directors had been attempting to work along the lines of a more participative management process for the previous six months. They had been moved towards this by the decision taken in principle by a large meeting of senior managers from the whole organization, including this unit. American consultants had run a seminar describing the advantages of participative management and of a consensus approach to decision making. The unit top team had attempted to implement the style described, and now felt that the managers below them should be given formal training for it as well—but not by the expensive Americans.

The three managers spent an hour setting out the firm's management history and their understanding of the present situation with care and clarity. They then asked me to describe the kind of training I would propose for the lower-level managers. I responded that I was not able to propose a training course. Their one-hour presentation had been most helpful in providing the general context; however it was not at all clear what the 'problem' really was, nor who had the problem. The real issues might not be addressed through a training course. It was essential first to look at the top team, rather than to propose training immediately for the levels of management below them. This review should concentrate on the realities of what was being attempted and what had been achieved so far. The actions and behaviours necessary to implement participative management should derive from the actuality of present behaviours, rather than focusing on the standard well-known skills of participative management which the unit 'ought' to be employing.

It is relevant to note that this group of three sponsors had made the same presentation to three other 'providers', all of whom had responded at the meeting with outline ideas of courses they would run for middle managers. The sponsors may have played a little game by initially expressing some disappointment at my comments about not wanting to run a training course for them immediately. They may have been testing to see how serious I was. The other consultants had what seemed to be good packages and could quote experience in using them. Did I really not know what the necessary skills were? At the end of the meeting, however, they told me that they wanted a proposal along the lines I had given them. Their reason for choosing me was precisely because I was the only one of four actually to say that a course might not be the right answer, and that middle managers might not be the best recipients anyway.

While the sponsoring trio were prepared to recommend this approach, they arranged for me to meet other senior executives and to discuss the proposed brief with them. A representative sample was chosen, including those who might be attracted to the idea and those who would probably be more sceptical or worried. An associated aspect, which was of course present but was not discussed between myself and the sponsors, was that this was another way of testing my personal acceptability to at least some of the group who would be involved, especially Colin, the unit director. In addition, there was discussion of the brief at a full top-team meeting before it was finally agreed and circulated to those involved by Colin.

It is interesting to contrast the process by which this brief was agreed by the top manager's team with the original edict from outside the unit which required a more participative management style—but which was itself a decision arrived at without participation! It is also important to note that, unlike some other areas similarly pursuing participative management within the organization, this unit agreed that the whole process should start with its top team, not with the middle managers.

The diagnostic phase now agreed upon involved individual discussions with 24 senior executives in two different countries. In addition, it was agreed that I should observe the top team at work in several of their normal management meetings. The individual discussions were based on a list of 10 topics drawn up following the original meeting and subsequent 'sample' executive discussions. Examples of the topics discussed were:

- What do you understand by autocratic and participative in the context of this organization?
- What progress and problems have you experienced in attempting to carry through the new principles agreed?
- Consider the managerial behaviour of your bosses: what do they do that helps or hinders you in the effective performance of your job?
- Consider your own managerial behaviour: what kinds of behaviour are rewarded, not rewarded, punished?

It had been agreed that the results of these diagnostic interviews would be given to the top management group in a specially arranged meeting. At the time, I was influenced by some recent experiences and comments from other consultants about the likely result of a written report to a group such as this on the kind of issues that were being raised. Although my normal practice would have been to write a report, on this occasion I proposed, and it was agreed, to give it orally. The prospective virtue of this was that it would thereby be possible in the first instance to present the report in terms of data, and to get comments on the data, without having to move on to the analysis and conclusions. The general idea behind this, which certainly seemed to be relevant in terms of a participative management style requirement, was that it would be more appropriate to consider the data and to generate discussion, rather than to move into the traditional consultant mode, which inevitably leads to the consultant being seen as the originator of the conclusions.

However, a participative style, whether for a consultant or for a manager, does not exclude a consideration of relevant political issues. Because of the major sensitivities that emerged from the report, a summary was given in advance to the unit director and to the personnel director. Neither of them attempted to influence the final report to themselves and their colleagues. The unit director said, 'some of your feedback is uncomfortable to hear, but we need to hear it'. The report was discussed by the top group in its three separate sections—data, comments and recommendations. The unit director illustrated the decision-making process identified in the report as one of the issues, by stating that the decision about the recommendations would be made by general agreement.

Given the major nature of the changes sought in the management of their unit, it is not surprising that Colin and his colleagues had encountered problems in trying to implement their good intentions in terms of participative management. Some of the difficulties they had experienced were as follows:

- There was disagreement about the meaning in operational terms of words such as 'participation 'and 'consensus'.
- While the nature of approved managerial behaviour had been clear and consistent although not articulated before, the 'now desired' managerial behaviour was neither clear nor articulated.
- While the top group had 'in principle' taken on the idea of participative management, there were differences of view about how effective this was proving to be, even within the top group. One management decision was quoted by some as an illustration of the new consensus approach; yet others commented that very same decision had not been arrived at by consensus.

In addition to the views of the top managers themselves, I identified a number of issues on which they needed to take action, including:

- The need for clearly defined decision-taking processes and definitions, for example the difference between 'I tell', 'I share' and 'we agree'

- The definition and acceptance of now desired managerial behaviour, such as openness, confrontation, explicit feedback
- The definition of roles within the new management structure which had now been decided

Discussion concluded with three main recommendations. The first was for a top-team workshop, the second that they should have an ongoing process consultant to help the top management group and indeed the management teams below it, and the third, that managers below this top level should have their own workshop based on the same principles.

The recommendations were dealt with in the terms set by the unit director originally; i.e., it was a 'we agree' decision. They decided to go ahead with a workshop for the top group, and to put the idea of process consultancy on one side for the time being; although they agreed in principle with the idea of middle-management workshops, a final decision on that was deferred until the top-team workshop had taken place.

The top-team meeting then decided to carry through one of the commitments I had made during discussions on the original brief. I had given considerable emphasis to the fact that this diagnostic stage was a stand-alone process. It would not necessarily follow that I would recommend any management training at all; nor would it follow that, even if I did, I would recommend or imply that I should be the person to carry it out. When they reached the decision in principle that they wanted to go ahead with a workshop for themselves, Colin asked me to step out of the room while they discussed whether they wanted me to implement this with them. There was some evident surprise among his colleagues, not that they should be making the decision there and then, but that I should be excluded from it. It is possible that my feeling that he was absolutely right to exclude me is influenced by the fact that I was called back almost immediately and told that they wanted me to go ahead with designing the workshop.

CASE 2

This organization provided the most prolonged and deep intervention in my experience. It was also my first intensive effort at very senior level, and I grew from the challenges, difficulties and frustrations it provided.

Change was a major feature of this organization—but it was change achieved through assault and battery, not through managed interventions directed through a change strategy. The case contained a series of projects, which were interconnected in that they started with one divisional director, continued with his group director boss and his divisional director colleagues, and finished with a project with one of his divisional colleagues. The introduction to two of the projects is described here.

Project 1

The first project started with a visit to a divisional director, Sid. The invitation to see if I could help him had arrived at third hand—from group personnel director, to manpower resources manager, to me. I knew nothing about Sid's division's activities, and the only comment I was given about him was that he was very bright, very demanding, and that I would have to prove that I could do something for him.

I arrived and was shown into Sid's office, although he was carrying out work with several managers and continued to do so and to speak on the phone for the next 20 minutes. He then rid himself of his subordinates, turned to me and said, 'You have five minutes to tell me why you think you can do something for me.'

I had been surprised but not particularly bothered by the first 20 minutes. My internal reaction to the five-minute sales pitch idea was that this was crazy. My response was immediate and unplanned. I simply said that five minutes would be a waste of time for both of us. 'Why?' I told him I needed to have at least some idea of what the issues were on which he needed help before I would be able to offer any kind of sensible suggestion. 'How long?' I had actually assumed that I would have up to an hour with him. (I now always ask or check.) I asked for 20 minutes, following 10 minutes from him about whatever it was that had caused him to invite me in. Sid launched with no further comment into a description of the issue on which he wanted help. This was, as I later came to find, characteristically crisp, eloquent, clear—and focused entirely on the performance of other people, not on his own behaviour.

At the end of the meeting, there was implicit agreement that I would undertake a project with him—in fact, he asked if I could come in the following week, which I could not manage. We settled for a few days later. I was asked to draft a notice to his colleagues setting out what the project would be. The draft was sent to him, but there was no immediate response. When contacted at one of his internal meetings by my boss he announced over the phone that 'the candidate had failed the written examination, but could retake it, with any help he needed. The notice was sloppy and some of it was unclear; try again.' There then followed some redrafting by me, further telephone conversations, and I was eventually accepted, with Sid making the point that there was a time specified for review after two months; plus, 'if it does not work out your consultancy suffers, not my division'.

The agreed project was spelled out in a note from the director to his colleagues:

Alan Mumford will work with the director and the X, Y, Z senior managers so that:

(a) the objective structure and interrelationships which will best meet the aims of X, Y, Z are identified and implemented;
(b) the interfaces between X, Y, Z and the other parts of the group are made fully effective.

In the first two months Mr Mumford will observe how X, Y, Z operates by being present throughout the day, first with the director and subsequently with each of the other managers concerned. He will be present at all meetings and discussions, but will not participate in them; he may make observations if invited.

At the end of this time he will report to the director on the results of this experience and a decision will be made on how to continue the project.

The first stage of this project took 31 days, including substantial observation of the director, and then discussions (not interviews) with his subordinate managers. The focus of the project derived from one of his comments in our initial discussion, in which he said that one of the main problems was that it always seemed to be him putting up ideas, and never his managers.

This was, of course, a luxurious process in the sense of the amount of time spent. The great virtue was that there was a mass of data, and, moreover, a considerable opportunity not only to compare observation with the view expressed by managers, but to establish a lot of concrete detail which I increasingly expected to be crucial in the eventual report to the director.

I had no structured format for analysing interaction at the meetings. Nor was there a set series of questions put to managers as I went round and saw them. I asked them how they could help me understand what the problems were. One clear majority view was that 'Sid will never change his approach.' I did not offer comments during or after meetings. Sid very rarely asked for feedback. I was happier emphasizing my role as listener rather than as consultant/helper at this stage.

The big issue was how the results of the project should be presented to Sid. He wanted a written report, and I knew from observation that it would attract his attention if it was brisk and erred on the side of certainty rather than obliqueness. We had had no kind of personal conversation, but I had picked up that he was a collector of aphorisms, and would dive into a file in order to produce some comment appropriate to a situation or problem.

Looking back, it is remarkable how little I felt I knew him after so many days watching him in action. Since one of the features of the report was to agree that few people presented ideas to him or argued with him successfully, I had no evidence of how he would treat my ideas. I went to three other people who knew him. A fellow consultant who had met him several times said, 'He is a nutcase—send him on a three week T-group.' Another consultant said, 'He is a bully. Hit him hard first.' My boss had said, 'Take him to Cambridge for the weekend and chat to him as you walk round the Backs.'

Since a number of the issues revolved around the unwillingness and inability of his managers to present, debate and/or discuss with him, I felt that the report needed to check out how he would respond to someone who, admittedly from a different relationship, did try that approach with him.

The diagnosis offered in the report ranged over objectives, structure, internal interrelationships and external relationships. It presented data first, and my comments, which I called 'Implications', second, before finally turning to 'Proposed Action'. Among other things, the report commented that:

- The Five Year Plan was not used to guide any of the decisions taken at this time. There was no business plan, merely a budget and a project planning timetable.
- Management performance was assessed purely on time or cost, not on any other issues.
- Most managers on most occasions seem to be present at decision-taking rather than involved in it.
- There were examples of upward delegation at all levels.
- Meetings held by the director with his managers were lengthy, were frequently dominated by his ideas and initiatives, had no shared objectives, and often undertook detailed work rather than reviewing detailed work.

In the report, I told Sid that I saw him as highly articulate, analytical, dominating, hyperactive, interested in detail, requiring immediate response to issues and giving no public sign of confidence in his subordinates. He was an impressive, authoritative public performer. Managers when dealing with him were less articulate, responsive rather than initiative-taking, rarely authoritative. There were few examples of managers advancing their own views in conflict with him. Sid relished one of the comments I included, that sometimes I saw him as 'a Rolls-Royce carrying vegetables', an observation which he several times quoted back to me with a question mark when he saw himself engaged in precisely that kind of activity.

The 'Proposals for Action' contained in the report started with the statement that the director 'should decide whether in principle he is prepared to secure improvements in X, Y, Z by trying to adjust the relative contribution of himself and his managers. The following actions presume the answer is yes.'

I wondered whether the combination of Sid's style and the unwillingness of his managers to offer more actually provided any prospect for development. I had no real clue how he would respond. Had he submitted himself to the really extraordinary process of being observed in action for days at a time, knowing that a report would be presented to him, because he wanted to improve—or because he found it flattering to have a permanent 'shadow'? On the whole, I gave him the credit of taking the risk of exposure.

Sid and I discussed the report off-site—at my suggestion. Characteristically, he had allowed two hours for it—and, also characteristically, he actually spent five hours on the main features. He then fixed another half-day because he was getting so much out of the discussion on the report—which was only four-and-a-half pages long. This underlines the relevance of the comment earlier about the mass of supporting detail which could be brought forward from observation and discussions. I returned to my office and told my (very worried) boss that the project seemed to be successful; he phoned his boss immediately to give him the 'good news'. Thirty minutes later, Sid phoned my boss to reserve my services for the continuation of the project.

Project 2

The results of the project with Sid were seen by his boss Herb, a group director. Sid gave him my report and Herb observed changes in Sid's style as a result of stage 2 of the project (see pages 73–75). Sid proposed to Herb that I should move into another project, this time with Herb himself and his subordinates. I knew that another person he trusted within his team had also recommended me. There were in fact considerable problems between Sid and Herb which I had observed in meetings between them. Sid told me there were other problems in Herb's team, and felt that if Herb had help it would benefit everybody. (An alternative view was that I would conclude that his boss was as hopeless as Sid thought he was.)

Herb had not seen me in action at all—he had only seen me as a 'shadow', and had amused himself by referring to an American radio play in which the major participant had been called 'the Shadow'. He quoted a line, 'only the Shadow knows'.

I went to see him prepared to discuss what I had done with Sid. However, a major feature had been confidentiality—i.e. that I would not pass on to others what I found out during the project—and this of course applied to what I could say to his boss! The line I took turned out to be acceptable; I said that the impact of the work I had done in X, Y, Z was presumably apparent to him from what he had seen for himself there and what he had heard from other people.

The proof Herb wanted that I could help him turned out to be quite different. He said that he was sure that I must have had an impact because he had seen a number of very helpful changes; if I could help Sid, I must be good! The question he then threw at me I had not thought about at all. 'Your work has been with British managers. I am an American with a different view of life, and your success with them does not prove that you can help me, an American. What makes you think you can?'

At that time I had never worked with Americans. I replied that I had relatives in the United States, that I had always been interested in American politics and had read US history as one of my special subjects at University. Growing in enthusiasm, I offered the view that there was no British person in the building who knew as much about American politics and history as I did. I did not have time to think about this fearful boast before he put his new question: 'Prove to me you do know a lot about American politics.'

From somewhere in my memory, unplanned, I responded. 'I bet no other British person in this building knows who Kissing Jim Folsom was.' 'So who was he?' I said he was a Governor of Alabama who had acquired the name through an addiction remarkable, even by American political standards, for kissing babies when on the election trail. There was a silence, then 'Can you tell which part of the United States I'm from?' I replied that I would say the East Coast and perhaps New York. 'I have lived mainly in New York since I was 14 years old; but I was born in Alabama.'

I got the assignment, which was:

To consider current perceptions held by Divisional Directors of the role of the Group Director, and the desired role.

This involved interviewing each of his colleagues and presenting their responses first to Herb, then to each of the other participants. They agreed or amended the summary of their general views, and focused their ideas on the main issues and the action that might be taken. This revised version was taken back for further discussion with Herb, and he circulated a written version of the second presentation. This was then discussed by Herb with each of the individuals separately and then in a group, with my presence at many of the individual discussions. Action was agreed, focusing particularly on the effectiveness of meetings—which involved a considerable period of process observation, and feedback on a behavioural analysis schedule to all the participants (see Chapter 5).

It will be noted that there was a considerable element of protection of individuals involved in this exercise. Herb was opposed to confronting all his directors in one meeting. He said, with some justification, that he had different problems with different individuals, and that he really wanted to discuss in a group only those things that were of general group application. That is why the eventual direction of the project turned towards the effectiveness of the meetings that he chaired with the divisional directors.

An interesting point about the process used here was the amount of oral feedback given through the first and second presentations before the production of a written report which was circulated to the whole team. The emphasis was on getting them to deliver and acknowledge their own views to each other, rather than producing an elegant consultant's report.

CASE 3

Some senior managers in a service organization felt there was a significant problem between head office and regional offices. I was invited to discuss with one of the top four managers how I might help. The idea of having a day in which problems and issues could be raised and discussed had already been suggested and widely welcomed. The idea of an outside helper had also been welcomed.

I presented three options. At one extreme, a day could be scheduled for setting out and clarifying the issues, which I described as 'Letting Off Steam'. As the analogy suggests, however, such an occasion can both relieve pressure and scald at the same time. Another major option was to move into a more intensive process, with objectives of team-building or organization development. This would involve much more serious diagnostic work to ensure that issues of real concern were identified and raised rather than concealed. Like the first-proposed event, it could be helpful at least at the letting-off-steam level. It could also be dangerous, particularly if there actually was no agreement beforehand on the objectives and also if participants got into issues of emotion and great personal sensitivity.

I proposed a third option, to be preceded by discussion with the four senior head office managers and some representatives from the regions on what the objectives and process would be for a one-day event. The discussion would also clarify the main issues.

This proposal was not discussed for four months. (I believe that alternative consultants were seen during this time.) When it did occur, it covered issues about the kind of problems involved in having a corporate policy but a supposedly decentralized management structure. It was agreed that the Group of Four would be the client, that a day should be designed for six months ahead. Meanwhile, four individuals representative of the people who would be involved would be interviewed, using a list of topics agreed with them. After the interviews I wrote to the Group of Four, setting out what I saw the prime issues to be, which would form the content of a workshop:

1. What you and your officers actually do, and how you arrive at the decision on what to do
2. The perceptions you have of each other's work and priorities
3. The interaction of the processes of communication, involvement and consultation, and the choice and success of each, for you and your officers
4. Clarity of managerial values and responsibility

I also identified a number of other issues which, I suggested, though important, covered too much ground for the proposed one-day event.

The workshop really continued this diagnostic process, because it clarified in greater detail some of the major issues that had been raised. We worked in three groups, each of which contained a mixture of the Group of Four, national officers and regional officers. (A decision had been taken not

to involve heads of functional departments at head office.)
The workshop proceeded through a set of tasks, setting out
the content for each discussion item. There were no formal
inputs. I acted as clarifier and facilitator for the day, and
prepared and sent to all participants a summary of the flipcharts recording the conclusions from their discussions.

The main issue that became a focus of attention on the
workshop was the question of 'being a professional' as
contrasted with 'being a manager'. There was not so much
ambivalence as downright opposition to this concept from
about a third of the participants. They did not see themselves
as managers, and really did not want to be managers.
However, on the whole the workshop was successful, with
perhaps another third seeming to shift their position during
the day, as they saw that a number of the activities that were
appropriate to their role as they saw it really were 'managerial'.

A month after the workshop, I met the Group of Four to
review the main conclusions they had reached (of which they
were reminded by the flipchart summaries I had sent them).
Three of the four felt that further action on the issue of
defining what they should be doing as managers was
necessary; however, negative views about the desirability or
feasibility of identifying and working on managerial issues
were expressed by the most senior of the four. Despite this, I
was asked to put up a proposal for further help.

In our discussion there had been some continued emphasis
on the need for 'management training'. (One of the four was
working his way through the Open University Effective
Manager course.) I suggested that management training
would not be a very worthwhile first step, since, until
individuals understood what they were supposed to do as
managers, working on skills would probably be unproductive.
The process proposed was to produce job descriptions for all
the participants on the workshop plus the heads of departments who had not taken part. This would involve individual
job descriptions for the Group of Four, but generic statements
for each of the national officers, regional officers and heads of
department. This would have the following purpose:

1. To improve individual manager performance
2. To improve relationships between managers
3. To identify individual and general developmental needs
4. To bring out any issues of organizational structure and
   working relationships which may affect the achievement of
   the first three aims.

There followed a delay of 15 months, caused by the decision of the top man to retire and prolonged arrangements for getting his internal successor (Alex) in place. Discussion then resumed on the proposal I had made, and the new project started, with interviews, one month short of two years after the original workshop, for what was now titled 'The Manager Profile Project', since there were objections to the term 'job descriptions'. A report was sent to Alex and his three senior colleagues four months after they had given the go-ahead for the project. It provided:

- The draft profiles as specified
- A review of the skills and knowledge requirements we saw arising from these profiles
- Additional comments on structure and working relationships
- Recommendations for development

The detail of the manager profiles is not important for this book; the relevance of the profiles was the part they played in encouraging the participants to recognize the range of managerial responsibilities they actually carried out, and through this to draw out the associated recognition that they needed some development process to help them meet these requirements.

The report additionally offered observations on:

- How the Group of Four seemed to operate
- Relationships between the organization and its members
- The 'hands-off' management style which operated throughout the organization
- The absence of strategy or objectives
- The relative absence of the conflict that had been the precipitating factor for the workshop two years earlier
- The prevalence of meetings
- The absence of effective teamwork
- The values of the organization

The report was initially discussed with the Group of Four, who accepted their own manager profiles which they had been asked to comment on in the drafting stage. They also accepted the generic manager profiles, with a few additions. They accepted the observations made, and explained why action was inappropriate on some issues upon clarification within the Group of Four. Finally, they accepted the recommendation for a programme based on the action learning principle of real work on real issues.

As the final stage of diagnosis and commitment, the report was sent in full to all managers involved, and was later discussed at a three-hour meeting with them. Alex launched the meeting by saying he wanted discussion on every aspect. He and the Group of Four felt that the recommendation for a development programme of workshops should be accepted, but he wanted full involvement of all participants in the final decision. There was serious and useful discussion on all aspects of the report, and the recommendations for a development programme were accepted. The programme started four months after the review.

Organizational Learning

I argued earlier that learning must be an explicit process for organizational learning really to take place. In the cases described in this chapter, learning as a process was an implicit rather than explicit feature in cases 2 and 3. The extent to which, none the less, these projects were in some measure contributors to organizational learning will be reviewed in Chapters 6 and 7. The next chapter reviews cases in which learning features as an explicit process and objective.

2 Can You Help Us Develop Directors?

This chapter moves on to diagnostic intervention designed explicitly for director development, as compared with interventions with the different purposes described in Chapter 1.

CASE 4

As with case 1, this was a large multinational firm. It was similar also in that it had arrived at some major concern about its performance—not, however, by direct comparison with competitors, but because of the threat of being taken over by a conglomerate. The take-over bid had failed, but it had stimulated concern within the organization at senior levels about the extent to which senior executives were equipped to handle increased competition, and the extent to which they might have slipped into a complacent view that they were almost automatically 'best of class' in terms of competition in their industry. The organization had a well established and apparently well accepted range of courses for managers, but not for directors of subsidiary companies. Some of these had attended external courses, either as managers or subsequent to their appointment as director.

The chief executive of the largest and most profitable company within the group was an advocate of more senior management development. The management training department already used occasional outside tutors on some of their programmes, but had not had a fully custom-tailored programme designed and implemented for them from outside.

These concerns within the organization coincided with the publication of a research-based study I had done on 'Developing Directors'. This had involved interviews with 144 directors in 41 different organizations. John, the management development adviser, read the report and called me in for a discussion. He was clear that what he wanted was a director development programme, that it would receive support at the senior levels in the business, that the needs it would meet could and should be defined more carefully. In the original discussion, John said the target population was new subsidiary company directors and even some who were 'about to be appointed'.

The 'Developing Directors' report (see Chapter 9) had set out a list of skills required of directors. We discussed the possibility of developing a programme based on those skill requirements, which seemed likely to apply generally in this organization. John, who already had some experience of defining specific needs within his organization, was as convinced as I was that this would be the least preferred option. The opposite of this was to do an aggregated analysis of a selected group of directors, identifying skills and working out the programme subsequently. Although John said he was in favour of this option in principle, in practice he did not want to accept it. The reasons seemed to be a combination of the probable costs involved and the fact that a similar analytical exercise on needs was going on at a lower level.

He therefore favoured my other option, a 'diagnostic workshop'. Although I would have preferred a more detailed analytical approach, I was happy to settle for this. A sample group of directors should work on the differences between managing and directing in the organization, and on what the issues were in their businesses, leading to a conclusion about the desired content of a future 'Developing Directors' programme. In addition, the workshop should illustrate the processes to be used, e.g. working on real problems (action learning) and working on how directors might learn.

John initially wanted a proposal for stage 2, the programme that would be designed after the workshop. Perhaps as a result of internal discussion, he decided later that we should go ahead with the diagnostic workshop, but leave stage 2 in terms of an absolute commitment until after this exercise. As in case 1, there was no doubt an element of testing out both the process and the consultant before committing himself to the final, more demanding, more risky and of course more expensive exercise of the full programme. In addition, he agreed to my suggestion that I should meet some of the directors who would be involved. Again, this gave them an opportunity to decide what they thought of me, while at the same time I was able to pick up valuable information about the organization's possible reactions to the proposed workshop and subsequent full programme.

The diagnostic workshop (which was not called that in the internal literature) was held with ten experienced directors. Four of them were managing directors of subsidiary companies, and, most excitingly, included the chief executive of the largest subsidiary, mentioned earlier as someone who had expressed the need for a director programme.

I found when I arrived for the workshop that John was far more twitchy about what had been set up than he had conveyed to me in any of our discussions. On the one hand, he was pleased at the level of participants he had attracted, especially the chief executive. On the other hand, if the event did not work, he would have wasted the time of some very important customers.

In fact, the workshop succeeded at all levels. The process used was found to be enjoyable and valid, and the issues, problems and skill requirements needed to bed the future programme in the reality of the organization were properly identified. The contributions of myself and colleagues during the workshop were found to be appropriate. The chief executive, whose strength and power within the organization were well known and obvious, contributed to the workshop in a delightfully balanced way which facilitated the expression of the broadest range of opinions about issues and problems. He had himself attended programmes at business schools, which perhaps explained but did not reduce the pleasure I gained from his comment in the final stages: 'I have never met a practical business school professor before.'

The virtues of a diagnostic approach were further revealed when the organization reviewed and accepted a list of content for the full programme which was different in several important respects from the provisional list I had suggested after our initial discussions. The detail of the differences is not important here. The significance is that it was the involvement of practising directors which enabled the identification of content that was more relevant and valid—and therefore likely to be not only more acceptable to participants, but even more importantly, much more valuable to the organization.

In terms of process, the most important aspect here was the acceptance of—and, indeed, in some cases positive excitement about—the idea of integrating work and learning. This diagnostic workshop illustrated directly the process of using individual learning styles as a vehicle for improved personal learning, the virtues of understanding the learning process in total through the learning cycle, and the idea that it was possible to integrate work and learning both in a day-to-day sense and through a major project. This latter was to be a major feature of the eventual programme. In terms of the comment made by my colleague about the limitations on my flexibility of approach (see page 3), the experience gained through this workshop is very important. The clear views I had then and have retained since in favour of basing such programmes on real work, real problems and explicit discussion of learning can be shown to rest on a firm base of acceptability to the customer and subsequent application.

I had been surprised when John had cut down the original proposal for a linked diagnostic workshop and director programme to a diagnostic workshop alone which would be a test of my whole process. I was confident in my ability to design and run a workshop that would lead to the acceptance of the full programme. However, the fact that John had changed his mind, either through his own worries or through discussions with other people, should have rung louder bells with me than it did at the time. I recognized insufficiently the limitations of his power. He had no authoritative figure—a group chief executive or group personnel director—who would say, 'this shall be done'. The course had to be charged out to the participating companies. John therefore had to persuade and influence a number of internal clients about the relevance and viability of the proposed programme. Whereas in case 1 there was a clear group responsible for its own development and its own decisions, in this organization there was no such group with decision-making powers for itself or for anyone else. In fact, the process John adopted was, as I discovered on my subsequent involvement, entirely sensible. To some extent, I had been misled by his original enthusiasm and apparent ability to 'get things done'.

As I was to find on many subsequent occasions, the question of who can say yes, and with what authority, is a major item of significance when it comes to acting on proposals for my interventions. This is especially but not uniquely true when the initial, and for a long time prime, contact is a management development specialist or personnel director. However, as I show in other cases, chief executives also sensibly feel the need to consult with those who will be most involved.

CASE 5

A colleague of mine had run an action learning development programme for middle and senior managers in an organization. The programme had combined work on a major forthcoming project with some more traditional inputs on various aspects of managerial and functional skills. The programme had been very successful not only at the level of immediate acceptability, but because the organization achieved the aims of the project, and believed that the programme had been a major contributor to this achievement. Ralph, the chief executive, in discussion with a colleague of mine who was responsible for the programme, had said that its success had revealed two new problems. He felt that the programme had resulted to some extent in senior managers being more skilled and knowledgeable than his colleagues on the board of directors. In addition, discussion of the issues raised while the project was being carried out showed that there were things to which they had given insufficient attention as a board. Although the tutors who had been involved in the programme had worked successfully with these managers, he rather wanted someone who specialized in director development to help him and his colleagues: did she know anyone who might be suitable?

I had not been involved in the design or delivery of the original programme. My colleague told Ralph that I had done the only research on the development of directors and sent him a copy of my book, *Developing Top Managers* (Gower, 1988). As a result, the three of us met over breakfast in a hotel in London. My colleague had told me that Ralph was a thoughtful, energetic man who had transformed the company from its previous state of likely failure. After appropriate pleasantries, and when I had just started to eat my bacon and eggs, he pulled out from under the table his copy of the book. He proceeded to turn to pages he had marked and ask questions about comments in it on appraisal, mentors, and the need for management development advisers to get close to the business—not the most digestible accompaniment to the meal!

We then moved on to discuss how I would approach the design of a programme of development for himself and his directors. In addition to the points already mentioned, he commented that the majority of his team were long in service in the industry, and in his own firm. The suggestion I made was for an approach I described as 'double value'. First, I would interview him and his colleagues individually. The purpose of these interviews would be to establish how well the board thought it was doing in relation to organization objectives, and also to draft a personal development plan for each individual. Ralph liked the individual diagnostic approach, and the combination of individual development and potential for total board development. He decided that he would go ahead; we discussed possible dates, and he asked for a formal proposal confirming the ideas discussed and potential costs. He said he would tell his board orally what was to be done—he did not think it necessary to write to them. He received the formal proposal within a week.

It then took some time to arrange a visit to the organization. In fact, a frustrating series of telephone calls proved fruitless until the chief executive finally returned one of my calls— three months after our meeting. He had now changed the nature of the visit. It was to include a 20-minute presentation from me describing my work with directors, and the alternative processes for undertaking a review of needs at board level. I should present the two alternatives of a diagnostic workshop (as in case 4) and the individual interview approach I had proposed. The prospective results—personal development plans and an identification of top-team needs—should be spelled out. Some examples of what might be done on a director development programme should also be given. After the presentation and general discussion, I would visit each director in turn to discuss their reactions and feelings about the proposal. This adjustment to the original apparent acceptance of the approach was preceded in the telephone conversation by 'I am not going to introduce you as my chosen solution.'

Clearly, the visit had been transformed from a confirmatory 'meet the troops' exercise to a more substantial sales effort. I was able to arrange the visit within a week of the telephone call. The presentation actually started late because of the absence of Ralph, who eventually turned up half-way through it. The questions and discussion were more positive than negative. Individual interviews afterwards ranged between a positive wish by the majority to 'do something' and an uneasy feeling by a minority that 'we are directors after all: should we really need something like this?'

There was then a further pause with no communication, then a telephone call from Ralph's secretary to say they wanted to go ahead, and discussing dates with me for individual interviews. When no letter confirming this appeared, I wrote to Ralph saying how pleased I was they were going to go ahead and confirming the arrangements that he would no doubt have confirmed if he had written to me! When I finally spoke to him, Ralph said that with one exception all the prospective participants wanted to go ahead with the project as proposed. The one exception was the personnel director, who had said that he thought the whole process was far too risky—how would the board and particularly the chief executive cope with any difficult issues which emerged from the general review? However, Ralph commented that these views only confirmed that the decision that the personnel director should take early retirement was justified.

The process of establishing personal development plans and the results achieved are described in the next chapter. At this point, the general report on 'Issues on Effective Development to Meet Board Objectives' can be discussed. The interviews were based on a list of 'Topics for Discussion', starting with 'What is your view of the major issues facing the top team?' The topics then moved on to a more direct review of individual needs.

The focus through objectives on what the board as a whole needed to do, and what individuals needed to do to contribute, produced a powerful blend. The General Report identified a range of issues requiring attention, including the fact that the substantial weight of experience was entirely within the industry; that, in terms of the Margerison–McCann team management roles (which they had previously completed), only the chief executive had an Explorer capacity; most of the others were Thrusters/Organizers. Yet the main emphasis for the future of the business was to be on diversification. The issues particularly requiring personal and group development included:

- Recognition of the difference between being a director and a manager
- The need for individual performance review for directors
- Shifting emphasis to directing the future rather than solely managing the present
- The need to develop more capacity for innovation in the top team in order to achieve the desired diversification
- More focus by the board on longer-term strategy
- Greater emphasis on corporate rather than functional responsibility

A useful additional input to the overall review was made following my attendance as an observer at two of the regular management meetings, in which it was possible to observe (and subsequently to comment on to the chief executive) the nature of the meetings, the kind of interaction involved and how this seemed to correlate with the issues arising in the individual discussions.

There was a delay of about six weeks before the report, and ideas on a director development programme, were discussed with the chief executive. We then discussed his own personal development plan, which he had had for several months, and the general report and reached conclusions on both. On the general report, he accepted all the comments, conclusions and recommendations and confirmed that he wanted to go ahead with the director development programme. He agreed to send out the report and the proposed programme to his colleagues. In fact, there was a further delay of a month before he did that, at which time the dates for the proposed first two workshops were checked with the participants. I have no note on whether the report was actually discussed by the chief executive with his colleagues, or whether he confined his discussion with them to the proposed programme.

Some points of special significance here include the possibility that the absence of a personnel director for several months may have contributed to the delay in taking action after the original report had been submitted. The new personnel director actually joined the organization after the chief executive's review of the general report and decision to go ahead with the programme. It may be that a credible personnel director committed to the ideas behind the programme would have encouraged Ralph to take action rather more quickly.

A second point to note is the extent to which, as an external consultant, I have to deal by telephone and letter with the apparent delays in making decisions, actually writing to the participants and so on, whereas an internal consultant would probably have been able to take more immediate personal action.

A third point is that several of the participants during the discussions had mentioned how valuable they found it to be to be able to make comments to an outsider, particularly as they knew they could make remarks in confidence knowing they would not be passed on to Ralph (or, if they were, only anonymously).

Finally, the good news about the involvement of a chief executive is that you can have no more powerful advocate. The bad news may be that an issue can be important but not be a priority for his or her attention in terms of actually getting things underway. The time that had elapsed from the first breakfast meeting to the commencement of individual interviews was six months; the first workshop of the director development programme was held a further seven months later. Ralph had originally said that the process could start within four months.

This was a particularly interesting diagnostic process for me. It combined for the first time (as I was subsequently to do more frequently) the double-value combination of a review of the general issues with personal development plans. With this particular client, however, there were the frustrations of shifts between an acceptance of proposals and a need for action, always followed by delays caused by the client. Until I got used to the fact that delay was a feature of this chief executive, the absence of action after apparent agreements produced concerns as well as frustration. Did he really want it after all? Was something else happening to make the project not wanted or not viable?

The delays struck one of the weaker points in my own behaviour: I do not like chasing other people for actions that they have accepted to undertake when they are clients. (I behave rather differently when I am managing people directly!) In addition, I had at that time some ambivalence about the extended initial process before commitment was finally registered. I was delighted when the chief executive said at the breakfast meeting, 'I want it.' When he converted the agreed subsequent visit into an additional sales process, I had two different reactions. Part of me wanted the chief executive to stick to the decision that I thought he had made. Obviously, it suited me better in terms of immediate commitment. Another part of me said that it was entirely sensible for him to consult with colleagues before taking on what was after all a very significant intervention. There is a difference between generating commitment to the answer in terms of identifying development needs, and generating commitment to the decision. The process I suggested made it clear to myself and others that I was absolutely committed to the idea of identifying needs through a shared process. I was not so committed at this time and in this case to the idea of shared decision-making before adoption of the process at all.

The Importance of GIGO

When computers began to make a serious impact on management information 30 years ago, managers sometimes learned painfully the significance of the message 'Garbage In, Garbage Out' (GIGO). The significance of the cases described above and in Chapter 1 is that they give a representative picture of my attempts to ensure that the interventions I make are based on real organizational problems, not on my presumption about what action needs to be taken with directors in 'any' organization. If a development programme is based on the wrong information, or indeed on a lack of information, it is not going to be effective in producing relevant learning. One of the great opportunities available from work at senior level is that it is possible to get away from the original Ford dictum that you could have any colour so long as it was black.

Lessons for the Learning Organization

One factor that emerges in many of the cases is the length of time it takes from initial discussion just to the diagnostic process, let alone to the implementation of a programme. With one exception (case 4), none of the cases here arose from traditional management development systems. Rather, they all arose from the identification of a particular issue or problem. To some extent, therefore, all but one of the cases could be defined as meeting the aim of organizational learning, which emphasizes transformational learning rather than incremental learning.

A further issue of significance may be recognized in the relationship between the urgency of myself as a consultant to get things underway, and the apparent initial eagerness of all of the clients similarly to get underway, and the causes of actual delays before things start to happen. Delay in most cases may have been due to the sheer pressure and volume of decisions faced by the most senior levels in an organization. However keen they may be on management development as a particular issue at a point in time, they are surrounded by other decisions which tend to push out the time-scale for decision on less immediate issues. It is my consistent experience that organizations will often ask for a very quick response in terms of a visit or the design of a programme, but that their own response is usually measured in months. To me, this emphasizes the extent to which we may have to accept that the real level of conviction about learning for particular purposes, let alone learning as a continuous process in an organization, is less powerful and immediate than many of us would like.

An even more interesting aspect of delay with especial relevance to the learning organization is the question of the nature of the decision-making process about such programmes. My own commitment to the idea of generating, through diagnosis, real commitment to the content of any process—whether it is producing job descriptions, an analysis of causes of managerial ineffectiveness or the design of a programme—will be clear from the cases described. Without the diagnostic process, and the delay in actually 'doing something' implied, I would not be able to do the kind of effective work I want to do. I recognize the impatience and disappointment I felt at the time about the other aspect of commitment. It would be very convenient if the chief executive were to accept my ideas and simply say that an intervention or programme should be set up. However, in only one of the six cases did the client actually make the decision on his own (case 2).

On the other hand, when the decision is shared, as in cases 1, 3, 4 and 5, there is much greater certainty for everyone about the acceptability of the decision. Decision-making by consultation and, indeed, explicit consensus can be a much more effective process—especially if the supposed management style of the organization is built around the idea of consultation and consensus. The frustration and irritation that I felt at the time and have revisited in reading my notes in preparation for this book are real. However, my overall conclusion is that, for work at top level, a consultative process of agreement before any intervention is likely to increase the chances of success.

Learning beyond Spoken Need

I have mentioned my colleague's ironic comment about my flexibility, which, however, always involved action learning and explicit attention to the learning process. Case 2 is the only one reviewed where explicit attention to learning was not part of the eventual activity; I had not identified it then as the crucial issue I now see it to be. My colleague's comment is well validated by the fact that in all the other cases learning as a skill or effectiveness requirement was never identified by the eventual participants. The *content* of, as distinct from the *process* of, learning was identified in most of the cases, but the process—how you learn effectively, just as how you might make effective decisions, or interview or communicate effectively—has never been raised with me as an issue.

How then do I justify its inclusion in the programmes I offer, since I give so much emphasis to meeting real needs through diagnosis? The answer is that I include it in my proposal to the client and explain why it is there. So far, all my clients have been interested and have agreed to include it. Perhaps I speak with particular colour, power and conviction on this subject! I am quite clear that it is impossible to think about using a work-centred process for helping managers to learn, and suggesting that the principles involved can be carried out after my intervention, without including serious work on individual and group learning.

3   Diagnosing Individual Needs

In the previous two chapters, the origin of the invitation to 'come and talk', and the basis of initial further work, was that there was a group of managers requiring help. Moreover, that help, it was envisaged, would be delivered primarily through some kind of group process, whether a course or a team-centred consultancy. However, not all requests for help have arrived or been delivered in that way. This chapter looks at how I assist in *diagnosing* individual development needs; the next chapter looks at the *content* of development plans.

Origins

Some features of the road I travelled towards the first major work I did on personal development plans are:

- A recognition of the fallibility of many general training courses as tools for the development of individuals
- An increasing awareness of the turbulent and complicated reality of the life of managers
- The discovery of David Kolb's version of the learning cycle
- Even more important (for this process), his identification of individual learning styles

This latter I can place with precision in 1976, when I first encountered and began to use the Kolb Learning Styles Inventory.

The other major feature taking me towards the personal development plan (PDP) approach was the Self Development Movement. This movement of the late 1960s and early 1970s itself arose from two slightly disparate forces. The first centred around views on effectiveness—that a great deal of formal management training was failing to help individuals because it was insufficiently grounded in individual needs. The second feature was a more philosophical and personal view—that individuals should be treated as responsible adult people who could and should create their own ideas for their own development. These two self-development propositions merged, since the latter proposition actually contained elements of effectiveness as well, i.e. that self-identified needs would be more likely to be grasped by the individual. I was one of the early UK writers on self-development—my first article on this was published in January 1972. I did not, however, develop those ideas in an authoritative and helpful way on a large scale, as did Mike Pedler and his colleagues John Burgoyne and Tom Boydell, through their excellent resource book, first published in 1978 (*A Manager's Guide to Self-Development*, McGraw-Hill, 3rd Edition, 1994).

CASE 6

In 1978 I began extensive work in one organization on *personal development plans*—a coincidence in time, but on reflection probably not a wholly accidental coincidence in terms of the direction of the management development world at that time. I was presented with the task of 'doing management development' with the top 40 executives in an organization, excluding the main board directors. The organization concerned had gone through a transformation of senior management organizational structure and, most importantly, of achieved bottom-line success. It had produced a corporate plan which proposed a doubling in size over a four-year period, largely by diversification and acquisition. The management development requirement derived from the view expressed in the corporate plan that, although the top managers were perfectly capable of continuing to run the business successfully as it stood, there was a need for development for the much larger responsibilities that at least some of them would have in the massively increased organization projected. The remit for me was to propose what should be done for these top 40 executives.

Relevant organizational history included the fact that there had been no use of external business schools, and that there was some junior and middle-management training but nothing that covered the top 40. The key executives (which is what they were called) held jobs around the world—in South Africa, Australia and the United States as well as the United Kingdom. There was an existing appraisal scheme, which was applied to, but was largely useless for, them. The appraisal document included reference to development needs, but the tiny provision of space allowed indicated how little was expected of managers who were completing it. The organization was very used to thinking of managers as individuals, because it was an early proponent of the idea of using psychological assessments as a major feature in the selection or promotion of managers. Finally, any suggestion of process and team consultancy work on management effectiveness, as carried out in case 2, was absolutely ruled out.

In addition to the general reasons encouraging me to think in terms of individual development, a series of informal interactions with managers at different levels suggested that two possible approaches to improved management development, i.e. via appraisal or courses, would not be acceptable, either.

The idea of improving the appraisal process to generate better identification of development would run into the need either to redesign the appraisal process entirely, or to risk being associated, through an improved 'personal development' page, with an appraisal process on which there was little conviction.

The fact that there had been little management training, and certainly none to influence the people I would be working with in this organization meant that ideas either of sending people on external courses, or of developing a major programme or collection of short courses internally were likely to be as unattractive to them as they were unconvincing to me. I proposed instead that we should establish individual development needs through a process separate from appraisal.

This proposal was presented first to the organization's personnel director and then to the Management Resources Committee (MRC), chaired by the chief executive. The proposal, with accompanying features which were very unusual for that organization, was in fact accepted with enthusiasm by the MRC. The enthusiastic acceptance of the chief executive was of course particularly important, not least because he used a variety of sources of information on the performance and interaction of managers throughout his organization. The personnel director was one of the providers of this kind of information—a fact well known to all the managers she visited around the world.

The personnel director, who was otherwise entirely supportive of my proposal, baulked at one aspect. The personal development plans were to be produced, as explained below, by means of a discussion between myself and each key executive concerned, before a draft PDP was produced for discussion with a main board director. I stressed the fact that this first discussion between myself and the key executive had to be confidential; the individual had to feel free to tell me things that not only would not necessarily be included in the plan, but also would not be revealed to anyone else, either then or at any other time. The personnel director did not agree with this confidentiality prescription, which I argued was crucial to enabling people to discuss things freely—which, after all, was one of the reasons for using an outsider rather than relying solely on the line manager. The personnel director wanted to have the information as well, and added that in any event the chief executive was bound to demand it. In fact the chief executive accepted the point and I was instructed to proceed as my proposal suggested.

Clearly, all 40 key executives could not be dealt with at once in the way set out below. So each main board director was asked first to nominate the individual whose personal development had the highest priority. Priority in most cases at this time meant likelihood of promotion, not perceived major weaknesses in performance. Work on these individuals was then followed with work on others, as awareness of and confidence in the process grew.

The Current Approach

This chapter deals with subsequent assignments in which personal development plans have been the prime objective of the process. (Case 5 in Chapter 2 involved individual and group development.)

The Process

A *personal development plan* is a document agreed between an individual and her or his boss. The version described here involved me, as a third party, in the original diagnosis of needs and identification of solutions.

The first step is the establishment of an agreement with the client on the nature, purpose and terms of reference for the production of personal development plans. A note setting out this agreement is sent to all participants.

Each of the participants is then asked to provide a two-hour slot for a discussion based on a set of topics. The 'pure' personal development version of topics (i.e. the version I use when I am not discussing broader issues) now suggests that the discussion proceeds through a review of:

1. Managerial experience to date
2. Own perception of current job requirements, skills, knowledge, competences
3. Own view on career plans
4. Own perception of development needs
5. Own perception of strengths
6. Own perception of areas for improvement
7. Development experiences to date

8. Development opportunities
9. Current work providing opportunities
10. Created work opportunities
11. Courses
12. Other suggestions

At the start of the discussion, I emphasize what they will already have been told in the briefing note, i.e. that elements of the discussion can be entirely confidential between the two of us (see case 6). I now give three definitions of levels of confidentiality:

1. You can quote what I am saying.
2. You can use this to develop the plan, but do not quote me directly.
3. Put your pen down: I am going to tell you something you should not even make a note of.

As a result of the discussion, I produce a draft personal development plan which the participants can correct.

Any factual error, or any point that they now do not wish to be recorded, can be excluded from the early parts of the report. Suggested opportunities for learning and development are presented as ideas for discussion between themselves and their boss, but it is pointed out that they are not committed to them. On this latter point, the participant is the expert on what should be said about past experience and own perception of skills, whereas I am expected to be aware of a wide variety of learning opportunities not familiar to most managers.

Individual Learning Styles

A major point is that development proposals for individuals vary not only according to the participants' needs, but also according to their individual learning styles., as discussed in the next chapter.

Other Diagnostic Instruments

Other people working on similar personal development plans use a larger number of diagnostic instruments. In my own case, I frequently add to the Learning Styles Questionnaire another Honey–Mumford product, the Learning Diagnostic Questionnaire. This enables me to bring in questions about skills of learning possessed by the individual, and also about the individual's attitudes and emotions as they may influence learning. It also brings out the absolutely fundamental question of the extent to which the organization encourages or discourages the individual as a learner. The details of the questionnaire are discussed in Chapter 10.

Otherwise I do not believe in adding to the number of questionnaires I ask individuals to complete. For PDPs, other instruments for testing decision-making or personality or other psychological attributes such as Firo B seem much more distant to me, not in terms of analysis of an individual, but of potential use for development purposes. It may be interesting to know what your particular make-up is on, say, Watson and Glaser Critical Thinking, or the Catell 16 Personality Factor. In terms of analysing developmental needs, however, my experience is that they are not very productive.

The Case for Third-Party Intervention

We may some day reach the espoused goal of many of us as management development practitioners, in which we have done ourselves out of a job. Line managers will conduct themselves with superb effectiveness in rationally, objectively and yet sensitively identifying and working on the development needs of their subordinates. However, I work mainly with organizations that have not yet reached this heavenly state. Some important person—in my case usually a chief executive or director, sometimes the personnel director—has recognized that the development of directors needs to be improved. They may be in the group mode identified in the previous two chapters; they may actually want to be or be prepared to be influenced towards an approach focused essentially on individuals. Whatever else they lay claim to, few directors and chief executives in my experience claim for themselves extraordinary skills or achieved results in this area. Many of them, indeed, tell me at first discussion how difficult they find it. So one motivation is simply to get something done. A second factor strongly influencing the use of an outsider is the negative feeling that they cannot use an insider. Either because of status, perceived competence, past experience or a combination of all three, directors often prefer to go to an outsider.

A further possibility would be to leave individuals to try and determine their own needs—a process that some variants of the Self Development Movement seemed to encourage. Unfortunately, most managers lack the analytical powers to undertake this kind of exercise on their own, even if they had the motivation. Even more, they lack an awareness of the potential range of developmental opportunities that they might be able to take up. They often fall back either on saying that perhaps there is a course, or that the last thing they want to do is go on a course and is there anything else available?

Of course, the use of an outside adviser can look expensive in terms of consultancy fees. The case for using one rests largely on the actual importance of people and the level of seniority described here.

Options on the Role of the Third Party

The purpose of the exercise is for a subordinate to agree with the boss what development action should be taken. The primary role of the third party is to make participants aware of their experiences, needs and options for development, pressing to the limits of self-perception. The third party needs to ask questions, occasionally to push and challenge. We are dealing with self-perceptions, and the familiar questions arise as to how accurate those percpetions are. The approach registered here causes those perceptions to be checked out with the third party but primarily with the individual's boss.

It would be possible to extend the range of discussion, to bring in additional views, for example of colleagues or subordinates. For those organizations that engage in upward appraisal, a contribution might be made from that direction. My own work has never involved that. Nor has it involved, for the projects described in this chapter, the use of feedback from the colleagues or subordinates in any other form. The basic proposition is that the individual proposes a self-analysis which is checked out by the boss.

I make no comment to either participant or boss on the self-analysis. My contribution to it is made at the time of the original discussion. I have occasionally encountered a complacent or desperately unanalytical manager whose self-analysis is extraordinarily restricted. It needs to be remembered that I have no means of knowing how accurate any perception is, although I can assess the range of issues being discussed, and how deeply they are gone into. I also have a modest amount of data which I would have collected about an individual during the discussion. The manager who claims to be highly organized, very well equipped to plan and very thorough in approaching managerial tasks, but who arrives for the discussion with no indication of having planned for it at all, provides disconfirming information which I will attempt to pursue by testing his or her proposed strengths in these areas. On the whole, my task is to facilitate participants to do the best job they are able to do of analysing themselves and presenting this analysis to their boss.

It has consistently proved very important to emphasize this point. I am neither a professional psychologist, nor even worse, an amateur psychologist capable of making quick assessments of people through an hour-and-a-half interview. I would regard such an intervention as being unjustifiable and intolerable even if it were acceptable. So I never make comments about individuals, either in the draft plan or in any subsequent discussion with bosses.

Which is of course one of the areas where the issue of confidentiality comes into play. 'Can we have a word about Ann before I have the discussion with her?' Of course I say yes. The subsequent discussion generally follows two paths. Fortunately, for most of my clients it follows the path in which the boss is trying to make the best possible use of the opportunity provided by this discussion, and merely wants to check out the procedures involved—how to start, how to finish. In some cases we then move on to rather more sensitive areas, such as 'Can you say anything about the expectations with which Ann is coming into the meeting?' My practice here is to refer only to information that is already available to the boss. 'As you know, Ann expressed some doubts about this exercise before we started. However, she did participate seriously in the discussion, and the plan does represent what she wants to discuss with you.'

There might be two realities of expectation underneath that statement. Fortunately, I have never encountered the wholly negative expectation in which I might, if I were to respond directly, say 'John thinks this whole process has been a waste of time', or 'John really does not expect to get anything out of this because he does not think you are serious.' I have worked with individuals with greater or lesser belief in the process, but never with anyone at those levels of disbelief. Equally, I do not see it as my role to tell a boss that her subordinate thinks that this is the greatest thing that has happened to him in the last five years, that he is very much looking forward to this discussion, but anyway thinks he has gained great benefit from the process so far. Actually, most of the directors I have worked with are much closer to this latter position; but I still do not think it appropriate to pass this on to the boss—I let *them* say it!

The only distance I would go on this was exemplified a couple of years ago. My director-client did want to know, after I had seen all nine of his subordinates, what they thought of the exercise before he saw all the individual plans. He had asked his management development adviser, who had picked up feedback from individuals about their responses and expectations. When the director met me to discuss his own individual development plan, he asked about my view of the responses of his people. I had been told in advance that some of them were doubtful about the exercise—and that he knew this; I suspected he had had some feedback from his management development adviser. My response was to say that it was for him to judge when he got to his discussions with each of the individuals. I added that it seemed to me that some who had started with a slightly cool attitude seemed to have warmed to the process. This had the great advantage of not particularizing, of giving him some reassurance, without clearly breaching confidentiality. 'Joyce didn't really want to do it, but now you should find that she liked it.'

Agreeing the Draft Plan

I do not now give participants the option of writing their own plans. My practice has been to say that I will do the draft for them because it saves them time and because, frankly, I am likely to be better at it than they are! My experience with trying to get managers to write their own personal development plans certainly proves that I do a much better job, at the level of both the detail they would be inclined to write and the range of options that they can remember from our discussion. In this particular context of relatively important people prepared to expend money, I think that the increased quality is justified. I recognize that it reduces the initial aspects of real involvement in self-development. However, that does seem to me to be covered at the two next stages, in which they can respond to the draft and amend it to their own liking, and in their subsequent discussion with their boss.

Generally, my experience has been that the drafts I send to managers are accepted with very few amendments. The comments I receive subsequently tend to confirm comments made to me during the discussion. 'I have never been given the opportunity to work through things in this kind of way before. It has brought out things I did not really recognize properly. Very illuminating and worth while.' Sometimes I have tripped up over a particular detail. 'I stopped working for X in 1981, not 1979'; 'I was actually quality assurance manager, not quality control manager—an important difference'. Very rarely do managers ask me to change the statements about strengths or areas for improvement.

On the occasions when a manager has wanted something taken out of my draft list of areas for improvement, my internal reaction has been that he has had second thoughts about the desirability of identifying it. I still believe this is most likely to be the case. However, I do recognize that I may have failed in my own listening, by overemphasizing a point made relatively tentatively in the discussion. Again, the important point is that whatever I drafted must be changed to what the participant wants to say.

In 15 years, I have never been asked to take out a point 'because that was a confidential thing I did not want you to pass on'.

The Final Stage of Diagnosis

The discussion between the participant and the boss is of course the crucial stage, although participants will often say they have benefited considerably even without the final discussion; they may say things like 'There are some things I will do anyway, whatever comes out in my discussion on the plan.' In case 6 I did take part (but purely as an option taken up by the participants) in the discussion between boss and subordinate on the draft plan, but I have never done this since. Bosses and subordinates have always chosen to carry out the discussion themselves.

From the point of view of emphasis on the reality of the discussion and on ensuring that responsibility is placed on the right shoulders, this is much the best thing. The weakness is that sometimes I know, from feedback from one or both parties, that the discussion has not gone as well as it might have done if I had been present as a facilitator. Another weakness is that, perhaps surprisingly, managers often fail either to make a note of the actions they have agreed on the plan, or subsequently to communicate the actions they have written down to each other. In fact, this weakness became particularly apparent with a client I had in 1992, as a result of which I have written into the guidance notes a statement that this should be the concluding part of the discussion: 'Boss and subordinate agree on who will take the actions following this discussion.' One of the reasons this weakness has emerged is that I draft the plan as a memo—I do not use a standard form. Of course, if there were a standard form there would be a nice blank space for 'Action'! But then it would look like a lot of other management development forms—and I want it to look like a piece of managerial work.

Does it Always Go Well?

Fortunately, most of the projects described in this and the next chapter were set up with the agreement of the participants involved—though they may have been given a strong steer by the chief executive. I have encountered reluctant participants, as described a little earlier. I am clear that a process of this sensitivity would collapse if it were a purely imposed process. As in many other fields, the capacity of managers to create a failure out of something with which they do not agree would probably show undreamed-of heights of creativity.

The main problems have arisen on the few occasions where there have been substantial differences of view between participants and bosses. In one case a participant had claimed a number of strengths, and had omitted references to weaknesses. The boss then found that, if he was to make sense of the exercise, he had to confront his subordinate on areas of weakness as well as strengths. I was then called into his office and given a very emotional tirade on how this process of mine had forced him into a position where he had to confront his subordinate on things that were difficult to handle, which he did not want to do, which had led to no productive result, and had only disturbed a previously happy relationship. He claimed that he had understood that the whole thing was about development, whereas he had been forced into conducting a mini-appraisal.

Undoubtedly, he had a logical point, although I suspected that the main difficulties arose because of his own failure in handling the discussion. I said that, since the discussion had clearly brought out points of significant difference between them, however uncomfortable, surely it was important that he recognized and dealt with the issues rather than with his discomfort. This was not an answer that he enjoyed, and he threatened to abandon the other discussions in which he was to be involved. Fortunately, one of these was with a relatively recent director, for whom there were development needs that were not of huge sensitivity. I persuaded him (drawing on the bank of 'I have been helpful in the past') at least to continue the discussion with this particular individual—his director of finance. That experience was indeed much more successful for both of them. However, the earlier problem was left unresolved. My discussion with both parties persuaded me that neither of them actually wanted to continue the discussion—nor actually, seriously to tackle the issues that had arisen. I made no further intervention. The two individuals survived—their managerial relationship apparently neither improved nor worsened by the experience.

Contribution to my Own Development

Perhaps I ought to be amazed at the presumption with which I proposed, designed and implemented the PDP approach in case 6. I had never done this kind of work at this level. I had been involved in very small-scale 'what to do after the course' exercises, mainly in my 'Trainer' existence. I had developed confidence in my ability to deal with senior directors through the quite different processes with which I was involved in case 2. It worked well in case 6—I helped the key executives there produce something that was meaningful, actionable and of benefit to the organization. A series of satisfied clients (even the irate director mentioned above) gave me more customers, and more general credibility for some other activities in the organization.

From my own wish to improve my performance, I did a complete review of the process—of the plans, of achievements to date. I shared the results with an external consultant, who made some useful observations on it. I cannot now recall whether I shared it with my boss, probably because I was going through a phase of shifting organizational relationships at that time; nor am I sure now whether I shared the results more widely in the organization, as a means both of proposing further action and no doubt of emphasizing the excellence of my contribution. What I am clear about is that I carried out the review—and that it proved to be an explicit part of my recognition of the use of the learning cycle. Strongly Reflector Alan was engaged in the reviewing stage!

I now recognize that, in that review and in subsequent reviews of similar projects, again largely conducted for my own benefit, I omitted an important element—personal satisfaction. I enjoy this work immensely, and am very pleased to take up or even partly to create opportunities to undertake it. It is an area in which, at least in terms of the measurement of my own criteria, I am absolutely sure that I do a good job, i.e. that people have draft personal development plans that are far better than they would produce on their own, or through appraisal or through any equivalent purely manager-centred process. I enjoy the process of drawing people out. I love the strokes I get from individuals who say how much they have benefited from the discussion.

I have only once had less complimentary feedback from a group I was working with. Perhaps it is significant that they were personnel people, because their comment was that the analysis of their strengths and weaknesses 'had not told them anything they did not know already'. I was surprised by this feedback because it was the first such criticism in 15 years. Perhaps they really had done self-analysis of the kind that I had taken them through, and really did find nothing new about themselves. More surprisingly, they expected me to add my own comments—which, as stated above, is something I explicitly ruled out in this as in all other PDP projects.

Relevance for the Learning Organization

Clearly, there are major limitations within a process that seems to be focused entirely on individual development, though it often of course involves interaction with others. PDPs are a useful but in themselves insufficient contribution to the learning organization. They provide experience for those involved in defining and working on learning plans. They therefore contribute directly, especially in my case with senior managers and directors, to the implementation of learning practices within the organization. They provide both leadership and role models for others to follow.

As in other areas of management development, it is much more appropriate to advocate, as many organizations now do, the advantages of personal development, the creation of learning contracts or learning agreements, if those at the top exemplify these processes in their own actions. The limitations of a purely one-to-one relationship—boss/subordinate—and the learning plans and processes derived from PDPs can be reduced if other developmental diagnostic work is done alongside the PDP. In the next chapter we look at such efforts, one of which has partially been discussed as case 3 in Chapter 2.

4 Individuals and Groups: Double Value

In its first formulation, the PDP approach was almost entirely individualistic. The personal development plan for each executive was the result of a self-contained effort between myself, the individual and the individual's boss. There was no reference in the first situation—case 6—to needs of groups of senior managers and directors within which this particular individual worked. The PDPs were explicitly unique; although some ideas of appropriate action might appear in more than one plan, there was no suggestion of action through which a number of individuals might be brought together.

This chapter describes how this original approach has been supplemented by the use of PDPs to assist in the generation of development activities for a complete group of directors, or for a subset. From the perspective of organizational learning, solo plans have the virtues of exemplifying the process, and modelling for others. Most senior executives in an organization have the power to give emphasis to learning processes, additional benefits are available at an organizational learning level where PDPs can be built into a process additionally focused on group needs. This chapter will describe such benefits.

Solo Personal Development Plans

The crucial feature of personal development plans in an organizational context is that, while the individual makes the initial analysis of need, the organization, in the particular guise of the individual's manager, takes the lead in making decisions concerning the accuracy of the analysis and the relevance and applicability of any proposed solutions. My PDP approach has focused increasingly on development experiences in and around the job, for reasons described in the Introduction. However, experiences occurring earlier than those recorded in this book included recommending whether a senior manager should be sent on the Harvard Advanced Management Programme. (He was, and subsequently became managing director.) As part of my own acquisition of knowledge for my role in case 6, I visited the then three major business schools in Switzerland, to add to the knowledge I had acquired ten years earlier through visiting Harvard, MIT, Columbia and the Wharton School in the United States; I also topped up my existing knowledge of the then three major schools in the United Kingdom—London, Manchester and Cranfield.

CASE 6

Because this organization had no significant experience of the use of major external programmes (or, indeed, of courses for the most senior levels internally), the potential use of external programmes was a matter of interest and debate—hence my tour of various business schools. In a few instances I recommended that individuals should attend a major programme, having previously conducted the review I mentioned and also having submitted a paper on the potential contribution of one or more of these programmes as a general feature of senior executive development. Case 7 in this chapter gives much more emphasis to other forms of development, but there are some interesting features of two particular PDPs in case 6.

A PDP for Steven

Steven was recognized both formally (the Key Executive Resource Plan) and informally ('Steven is going to finish up as managing director') as a high flyer in the organization. Before my involvement he had been put through a series of management posts, largely as the need arose to fill them, but with some general idea of testing him out and with an even more vague idea that it would help with his development (a phenomenon I have subsequently described as the Big O— giving somebody a big opportunity, but no real guidance on how to convert opportunity into achieved learning). There was absolutely no hesitation about placing him on the PDP list—all the important decision-makers agreed that he ought to be given further development.

Steven, a relatively young man, was general manager of a subsidiary company, and worked for Tom, who was chairman of a group of companies. My first discussion with Steven brought out one of the most overt issues of confidentiality that I have ever encountered. He had listened to my statement about this issue without making any observation, but when we got to discussing his development needs in more detail he asked me to confirm that I really meant what I said about confidentiality. On further reassurance, he made a statement: 'The best thing you can do for me is to give me the opportunity of working for a different boss. I cannot tell him, and you must not tell him or anyone else, but I have absolutely nothing more to learn from him—and I am finding it increasingly difficult to conceal that I do not really think he is very good at his job.' There was actually, even without this statement, good reason to give him a different kind of experience, and in the early stages of work with him on the PDP, and in discussions with his boss and grand boss, this could be discussed without breaking confidentiality. He was in fact moved.

I mentioned earlier in this book that I am a user of irony and a collector of ironic and paradoxical circumstances. Tom agreed a retirement date for himself. At the same time, it was decided that Steven would succeed him. It was also agreed that, as part of his final preparation, he should attend the then well regarded Harvard course held at Vevey in Switzerland. All the participants in planning agreed that because of the nature of the job it would be extremely difficult for Steven to attend the course after taking up his new post, even if this had been regarded as the best timing. The difficulty was that Tom was going to retire, and be succeeded by Steven, before the starting date of the Vevey course.

Now I encountered an ironic situation the particular flavour of which only two of us could taste. Tom, without any prompting from the chief executive, volunteered to delay his retirement by four months so that his successor could attend this course. Only Steven and I could savour the irony involved in Tom giving up a retirement date (fixed incidentally quite a long time before and involving a world trip as a retirement present to his wife) to help someone whom he saw as a protégé but whose views on the qualities of his supposed mentor had become increasingly harsh.

I too had seen the divisional chairman as an extremely pleasant but relatively ineffectual individual. Tom had had no formal management training himself, no experience of sending anyone else off for management training; he had no connection with the business school—no alumni association preference. He surrendered something important to himself and to his wife in favour of the man who was going to take over from him. There was no reward for him at all except the sense that he was doing the right thing for someone he regarded to some extent as his protégé.

Looking back, what strikes me is the effective combination,

which I doubt I recognized at the time, of decision-making on a wholly rational basis and more emotional, personal, issues for one of the participants in the decision. The PDP approach provided the rational basis for the decision, and certainly the decision would not have been taken without the PDP. Even if the organization had taken aboard the general desirability of a senior executive course for someone in Steven's position, it is most unlikely that in the particular circumstances he would actually have been provided with the opportunity. It was the detailed analysis provided through the PDP, and the fact that this was shared by Tom, that convinced Tom subsequently that, not only was the Vevey course the right answer, but it was one to which he should contribute at some personal sacrifice. I have never since encountered a decision involving such personal generosity.

The lesson I draw now is that, whether we look at the case as purely involving personal learning, or as leading towards a learning organization, personal relationships (even though in this case founded at least partly on an incorrect perception) are often major contributors. The learning organization is not just a system for a collection of statements, policies or procedures: it is the live interaction of individuals. Case 6 demonstrates in a rather odd form the crucial commitment of one of the required features, not just in personal development plans but in any construct purporting to enable organizational learning to take place. In nearly all circumstances, an individual's boss is the most potent of the people through whom he or she will secure access to learning opportunities.

Of course as I show in detail in my book on this subject (*How Managers Can Develop Managers*, Gower, 1993), providing access as the divisional chairman did in case 6 is only one form of help—though it is the kind of help most senior executives recognize in traditional management development schemes. The unusual feature of this case, apart from those already identified, was that the boss here really had nothing to offer other than access. We would certainly hope that most bosses in most situations could provide a much more personal developmental relationship. The next example shows the much wider range of possibilities that are available through a personal development plan.

A PDP for Bill

Although this is an example of a purely solo plan, it actually emerged because of my involvement with the organization described in case 4. As a separate project, but because of the work I was doing with the firm on a director development programme, I was asked to help produce a PDP for one of their senior people. The main features of the PDP are shown below:

Managerial Experience

His experience has been in engineering, production and project management.

In addition to a variety of offices and works in the UK, he has had assignments in South Africa and Denmark. He is currently general manager of a £10 million turnover company, and has held that position for three years.

Personal Experience and Development

He thinks the main areas missing from his experience have been product development and marketing. Although he has not worked in finance or human resources, he feels his experience with these has been secured through the jobs he has held so far. Similarly, because he was involved in actually selling a number of project management contracts, he thinks he has developed a number of skills in selling and project management.

However, the area he identified as being most important to him at the present time is that of strategy. He took over a company with a well organized business plan in a context of relatively secure markets. However, he believes a change is likely to occur as the environment is going to become much tougher in the next year or so.

Possible Development Needs

• Marketing
• Product development
• Finance (despite the comments made earlier, he recognizes the need for higher-level financial knowledge)
• Role of a general manager (he is not always sure of the level of detail at which he should operate, the use of network within the group, and generally what should be expected of him)

In addition to these functional areas, he identified a few skill areas in which he feels he might be developed:

• Setting clearer targets and objectives for people
• Selection skills, especially interviewing
• Team management
• Dealing with customer problems

Possible Development Processes

His scores on the Learning Styles Questionnaire (LSQ) indicate that he has a strong preference for the Pragmatist learning style and also the Reflector style. He scored a Moderate level on the

Theorist and Low on the Activist. Discussion of these preferences show that the scores on the LSQ correctly identify his own perception of his approach to learning. He has, for example, been on several courses which he criticizes strongly in retrospect because they seemed to have nothing to do with the industry in which he worked (Pragmatist). He has also recently turned down an opportunity to go on an outdoor course, perhaps not surprisingly, in terms of his Low scoring on the Activist dimension.

Learning-centred activities that might be attractive to him include:

- Involvement in some industry-wide committees on which he does not currently sit, where he would be exposed to more marketing and product development issues
- A planned series of discussions with the group finance director and his divisional director, going over some of the proposed new financial reporting arrangements
- An interviewing skills course, which would not necessarily have to be industry-based
- Preferably a substantial visit of two or three days to the Group Business Strategy department, provided that clear objectives and end-results could be defined. This should be preceded by recommended reading
- The fundamental issue of what his role as general manager is should be covered by some recommended reading, and some arranged visits to three other general managers in the group

This is an abbreviated version of a rather fuller document, but it contains the essence. Further discussion on some of the features exemplified in this PDP is provided at the end of this chapter; and Chapter 13 describes the application of learning styles in more detail.

Group-related Personal Development Plans

I have increasingly used the double-value process described in case 5, in which needs for the development of directors as a group is achieved through a diagnostic process which covers both the production of personal development plans and an overall assessment of group needs. Case 7 describes some of the elements that emerge from this kind of initiative.

CASE 7

This case has not been discussed in the earlier chapters, which dealt with the entry point for an organization. It is covered here now because it is particularly relevant to the question of how PDPs can lead to a wider group or organizational diagnosis and then to action.

I participated in a conference the theme of which was 'The

Line Manager as Developer'. A substantial part of the conference seemed to me rather removed from the apparent intention of the conference, because the cases presented dealt mainly with how line managers had been involved in designing and redesigning appraisal schemes, or changing the content of management training courses. In the afternoon, however, one of the major contributions was made by a management development adviser, who described his attempt to get managers to take more responsibility at a personal level for developing themselves and others. At the time I was writing *How Managers Can Develop Managers*, and wanted to get illustrative organizational material. I contacted the adviser subsequently to ask if he would be prepared to talk to me about their approach, which actually was being focused through an organizational effort to get managers to produce personal development plans.

He agreed to see me, and we had a useful and interesting discussion, which was in fact helpful for the production of materials for my book. At the end of the discussion, he asked me to say something about my work at director level. He then revealed that the reason behind the question was that, although PDPs were being produced at middle-management level, so far they had not been successfully prepared by senior managers. One director, Tony, was interested in doing some-thing, but he and the adviser both felt that an external resource would probably be necessary to secure the necessary credibility at senior level.

I met Tony and he accepted my PDP process, including the production of a PDP for himself. However, he wanted this aspect to be twinned with questions that would test a document recently produced describing the competences required by managers at this level. This document had been 'agreed' at a management meeting between him and his senior managers. He now wanted the list of competences to be checked out through discussion with the managers, and he also wanted some observations from an outsider on the accuracy or completeness of these competences.

Discussions then took place along the lines described earlier in this book, in which a section of questions related directly to personal development (see p. 34) was preceded by a section dealing with the other issues:

- What do you see as the main opportunities and problems facing you as a manager over the next three years? (See the notes produced at our meeting on 12 July)
- What skills, knowledge, personal characteristics do you

believe will be necessary in your job to meet those opportunities/problems?
- Would you add to or subtract from the attached list of senior management competences?
- Do you see significant differences between your job and those of your senior colleagues in the division?
- What are the main dimensions of your job—budget, people?

In addition to these topics, a further issue was raised during discussion with Tony on his own personal development plan. He referred to an aspect of relationships between himself and his senior managers, and asked that during my discussion I should get feedback from his colleagues on this particular issue.

The PDP contributed to the identification of development needs for individuals, for the group as a whole, and for a subset within the group.

The group as a whole commented on the senior management competences that had been produced, and these comments were accepted. There were some differences of view about priorities, but no generally agreed additions to the competences. However, I suggested that they should consider three additional competences.

On the particular issue of feedback to the divisional director on the aspect of managerial style, about which Tony was concerned, the feedback from participants partly allayed his concern, but partly confirmed it. Perhaps the most interesting aspect was that most of the participants claimed that they saw others behaving to the divisional director in a particular way, while they themselves—uniquely—did not.

When I gave Tony this feedback, he expressed disappointment not with that feedback, but with the absence of more general comments. He now wanted feedback on all those aspects of his interaction with his managers that I might have picked up in discussion. I agreed to review the data and let him have more information, but commented that this would not be as valid as the feedback I had explicitly sought. Perhaps I should have anticipated an additional request of this kind, and prepared myself for it at the discussion stage. However, in my opinion it would have been inappropriate to extend the basis of the individual interviews to a total view of his style, since this was neither the main theme nor something for which Tony had asked at that stage.

In the report covering all these issues, I suggested a linked programme of three workshops covering:

1. Developing Myself and Others (including work from the personal development plans)
2. Innovation and Managing Change
3. Creating an Effective Team

Discussion proceeded between Tony and the individual managers on their draft personal development plans. Parallel discussion took place between him and the company's personnel director on the report, its feedback and recommendations. As a result of this and a discussion between Tony, his management development adviser and his managers, a workshop was held on 'Developing Myself and Others'. It was thought this was the most appropriate follow-up to the personal development plans—which, indeed, were reviewed at the beginning of the workshop.

The good news was that the workshop participants, who were put in pairs to discuss their experience on their PDPs, reported that they had benefited from the process. Several of them told me privately that the whole thing had gone much better than they had expected when the project had been set up—there had been some concern about how serious Tony was.

Three other points that emerged from the workshop are of special relevance to the theme of this book.

Sharing Information   Each of the participants had completed a Learning Styles Questionnaire and a Learning Diagnostic Questionnaire (see chapters 10 and 12) as part of the PDP process. They had received feedback and explanation on these. The divisional director had not only received details of the results and interpretation in each PDP but had been given, as an appendix to the general report, a copy of all the results and the general conclusions arising from them for the group as a whole. However, I had asked that this appendix should not be included in the general report when it was circulated to the whole group, because they had not been asked to share this information with each other at this stage.

Since I had rather congratulated myself on the punctilious approach I had adopted here, I was more surprised than I should have been by some feedback immediately prior to the subsequent workshop. The preparatory note I sent to participants said that I would be asking for their approval to share the results within the whole group. I then heard from the management development adviser that the most senior manager in the group objected violently to this. He had said that they had been told that the discussions with me were confidential, that information delivered to the divisional director was one thing, but to share it with all his colleagues was another, and that my request for their approval to share the results was essentially bogus since there was no way they could publicly say 'no'.

In other groups in which I had shared such information, there had always been interest and fascination, not objection, and no doubt I had come rather too easily to the view that these people would want to share. I said at the workshop that I had heard there was concern over this request and therefore I was dropping it. Tony, whom I had warned in advance on this issue, said that, since people were worried and since he had the information anyway, he agreed that participants should not be forced to share it; 'but, just to show that there could be value in doing this, here are my scores'. He then gave his own High and Low scores and asked the group to bear these in mind as he responded and acted during the workshop. In addition, I had seen the main objector before the workshop began, and had told him what I proposed to do.

During the first morning it became clear that this particular issue represented concerns by two or three participants about the level of openness and trust that could be managed. In effect, the participants seemed to me to be placing themselves in a double bind, because they were saying they were not prepared to be fully open and trusting, especially in relation to their boss Tony, until such time as they found that they were not going to be punished for being open about issues. However, since they could find that out only by actually raising issues, the point might never have been resolved! Gradually, however, the difficulty was overcome, partly through leadership from Tony, partly because I made it clear that the issue was within their control to experiment and to test the reaction of the divisional director. Fortunately, by day 2 the main objector, who had been rather silent during day 1, became an energetic and helpful contributor, and indeed finished by taking the lead on another matter.

This was not just a general issue about openness and disclosure, which might occur in any kind of management development workshop; it was an issue specifically about disclosure of information about learning—which not only was the theme for the workshop, but of course was of significance to the further development of this group as a learning group.

Tasks and Learning   A second issue of especial relevance arose from my general report and from several personal development plans. The division had set itself the target of becoming world-class in its area of work, and I had suggested that several of the participants should pick this up as a combined task and learning project. During the workshop they really caught on to this idea. In addition, they proposed an additional project for themselves, concerned with some current employment issues. They explicitly stated that they would set the project up and run it themselves—without the direct involvement of the divisional director.

Extending the Learning

The third issue of some significance was a commitment raised by participants, and agreed as part of their general action plan, to take through within their own units the kind of process and activities that had been taken through with them on personal development plans and the content of this workshop.

It will no doubt be reasonably clear that all three of these issues impact directly on relations in a learning organization. People must be willing to share data among and about themselves—but they must be in control of that sharing. Perhaps, in a group workshop that focused visibly on learning and development, it is not astonishing that they themselves took up the idea of an additional task and learning project— but there is significance in the fact that they took aboard the principle of working through an existing task and converting it into a group project instead of an individual managerial task—even though the workshop agenda did not ask them to do this!

Planning the Action

One significant weakness occurred at the end of the workshop, which paradoxically reflected the good news about these managers wanting to take charge of their own development and their own actions and their own project. They explicitly declined the opportunity to have a final action planning session, in which I would have helped them neatly to record what they had committed to do. The divisional director, who had been making notes throughout the workshop, said this would not be a problem for him since he had recorded his own action points. It later transpired that in fact he had 'lost' at least a couple of the agreed actions, so I sent him a copy of my own review notes with all the actions set out.

In one sense, this feature is not uncharacteristic of many management meetings, where actions are not properly recorded and sent to all participants. Certainly, my own normal style is to cover this aspect very carefully, and I now recognize that I should have found a way of carrying through the action record without at the time explicitly contradicting their wish to 'look after actions for themselves'.

A Note on Timing
My letter to the management development adviser in this case asking if I could see him to talk about his approach to personal development plans was dated 2 July. The timetable thereafter was as follows:

1. Discussion—management development adviser—two weeks later in July
2. Discussion—divisional director—October
3. Decision by divisional director to go ahead—'in principle'—December
4. Formal agreement and confirmation—end of January
5. PDP interviews—February
6. Agreement of draft PDPs—February/March
7. Submission of general report to divisional director—March
8. Discussion with divisional director and personnel director—March
9. Workshop—July

Again, one of the issues here was the very sensible desire of the divisional director to ensure that his managers understood why he wanted this process to be set up, and to get their commitment to the eventual decision to go ahead. There were one or two people who were doubtful at the beginning of the project. The position of the insider management development adviser here was important, as he collected views and opinions and sought to allay some of the concerns about whether lifting the lid on some issues was going to be helpful to the group as a whole.

The Right Solutions?
The issues brought out through the PDP approach, whether used solo or in a group-focused effort, bear the same features. Any solutions have to be realistic as well as valid. They have to:

• Meet organization priorities (which rarely place organizational, team or individual learning high—would it have taken this division eight months to get into action on a work priority?)
• Meet personal priorities, in terms of the kind of effort individuals are prepared to put into learning and development, and the issues on which they feel most strongly in terms of their own development

- Take into account organizational culture and history, which may influence the kind of solutions that might be appropriate—Harvard for everyone, an away weekend, action learning projects?
- Consider the opportunities actually available, especially for learning from real work (see Chapters 8 and 9 for examples)

The other crucial endeavour is make sure that all learning processes give people the chance of going fully round the learning cycle.

In addition, the individual issues brought out through the Learning Styles Questionnaire and the Learning Diagnostic Questionnaire, which help to influence the extent to which any individual will take full advantage of any particular opportunity, can be built in. Will this individual *learn* from an outdoor experience, as distinct from being stimulated by it? Would this individual benefit from a three-day high-powered course at the London Business School? What kind of emotional risks will this person be prepared to take in participating in a task or a learning activity?

5   From Diagnosis to Action in Groups

The previous chapter reviewed the introduction of personal development plans in the context of whether they were used purely 'solo' or were carried out as part of a group process. This chapter looks at a variety of experiences explicitly focused on action to deal with group needs. The cases are referred to in a chronological sequence. The sequence represents a shift of focus, from task and process issues as the basis for intervention, to a focus on learning through task.

In case 2 (project 2) and case 8, intervention was geared to facilitating improvement of task by the illumination of process; learning was never an explicit objective for either the participants or myself. I could claim that learning was an implicit aspect of what was occurring, and I could certainly claim that in some senses learning must have been achieved because there was a change of behaviour. I now see that I missed opportunities to suggest learning and development as objectives in their own right, and missed the chance of introducing procedures that would have made this additional benefit from process intervention both more clear and more likely to be achieved.

In the later cases (1 and 4), development was the explicit intention, rather than an incidental and unacknowledged by-product. In both cases, the centrality of real tasks was a major feature in the design of programmes. However, the real tasks involved were captured and in some sense isolated for the purposes of the programme, rather than there being the constant focus of attention on the relationship between task and process.

CASE 2

Project 2

In this project the client was Herb, the American main board director with whom I had shared knowledge of Kissing Jim Folsom (see Chapter 1). He had decided, after discussion on the initial diagnostic feedback, that, in addition to work undertaken with each individual, he wanted to make the general meetings he had with his staff directors and divisional directors more effective. In order to contribute to that, it was agreed that I would change roles, from being an interviewer and collector of data, as I had been at the first stage, to being a process observer at the meetings. I used a framework for this drawn from a variety of sources but particularly from a book, *Discovering Interactive Skills*, by P. Honey, N. Rackham and M. Colbert (Wellens, 1971). (I had not then met Peter Honey.) This enabled me to note the contributions made at meetings, so I was able to give feedback on who was doing what, in terms of oral behaviour.

Among the observations I made after the first meeting were that:

- Proposing behaviours came almost entirely from one of the four directors involved—and it was not Herb.
- In $5\frac{1}{2}$ hours of observation, there were no 'building' behaviours.
- Half the 'disagreeing' behaviours came from one person.
- There were eight 'digressions' from the agenda or topic under discussion, all of them from one director.
- In the $5\frac{1}{2}$ hours, there were only three summarizing comments.

In agreement with Herb, a copy of a detailed analysis of all the behaviours at the meeting was circulated immediately afterwards to each participant.

It is extraordinary to me, looking back, that I did not provide, nor did any individual ask for, group discussion on this feedback—though several, including Herb, talked to me individually about the analysis. I commented that there had been no minutes, no time control, no agreed agenda. I did a general review with the group director after six meetings, collecting all the observations I had made. The 'proposing' items continued to be dominated by two people; there was no building or encouraging; and disagreeing comments tended to be dominated by two individuals. The 'informing' category was dominated by the divisional directors—Herb practically never presented information from his own level.

I gave them a questionnaire on the effectiveness of their meetings, derived from my discussions with them. The results of this are given in the next chapter.

This behavioural measurement was only one aspect of a much broader project, which for example looked at issues such as the extent to which they were almost totally dominated by short-term fire-fighting and crises. As I commented to them, they were heroically attempting to put right last week's mistakes, instead of aiming as directors to think sufficiently far ahead to prevent mistakes occurring. In one sense, of course this can be seen as an implicit contribution to learning—because individuals and the group of directors as a whole acquired data about themselves which enabled them to take action to correct errors.

The group established for itself, with my help, ideas on individual and group behaviours which would lead to an improvement in performance. However, discussion of what was actually going on was extremely limited—to 'special occasion' meetings in which 'Alan's feedback' was discussed. What was missing was more substantial periods of analysis, reflection and construction. It was largely a case of individuals, and especially Herb, who received a lot of personal feedback from me, deciding to 'try and behave differently'. This project was perceived as valuable by the participants, as was illustrated by the fact that I was involved with them over a considerable period of time on a variety of issues associated with their performance as directors.

Now I feel less proud than I did then about the effectiveness of my intervention among a group of tough-minded, egotistical, task-focused directors. What I achieved was too much of a one-off experience related to the specifics of particular aspects of their behaviour. It was insufficiently integrated with more general considerations of how they could apply this particular experience to the generality of their behaviour outside these meetings. The good news was that they got what many of them claimed to value at the time—objective data from an unbiased source. I now feel that, though this was indeed a strength of the exercise, the fact that we never discussed it as a group, as distinct from my regular individual discussions with Herb, meant that they were not required to think hard enough for themselves about what was actually going on.

Perhaps most crucially in terms of our understanding of the learning organization, this case illustrates that the creation or evolution of effective management or organizational systems and disciplines can lead to greater managerial effectiveness, without seriously contributing to the creation of a learning organization.

CASE 8

The organization described in case 6, in contrast to that in case 2, had explicitly wanted me to focus on individual development. Indeed, I was told firmly that the experience I had had of process consultancy, though important in terms of establishing my credibility for senior management work, was not to be offered in this organization.

It was therefore ironic that I was later asked to carry out a process consultancy exercise for another company in this organization. Hank, vice president of the American subsidiary was impressed with the work I had done on personal development plans for some of his subordinates. He asked my boss if I could work for him on building team effectiveness.

Hank spent some time briefing me on the nature of the problem as he saw it. He thought his subordinates generally tended to act within their own separate functions or managerial responsibilities. Even more specifically, he thought that the regular meetings he held with them were much less productive than they should be because people simply did not interact; they were not creative in thinking of ideas for improvement or encouraging of each other in meetings. He told me that they all seemed to operate separately, and seemed unwilling to help him when he tried to draw them into discussion or consensus.

I went to the United States and sat in on a management meeting. As I found from my observations of this and other meetings, and from discussions with Hank and a number of his subordinates, there were a number of reasons for this lack of interaction. However, there was one major cause, which could be put right with few of the agonies of introspection, data-sharing, definition of criteria for effectiveness and the deliberate creation of an atmosphere of openness and trust so beloved by many of us who saw ourselves as working in the organizational development mode.

The meetings were held, unsurprisingly, in the board room. It so happened the room was relatively long and narrow, and was occupied by a long narrow table. I observed immediately another extraordinary physical characteristic. Hank sat at one end of the table, with four of his subordinates, two on each side next to him. There was then a long gap to the other end of the table, at which sat another four executives. As I observed the meeting, it became increasingly clear that for considerable parts of the meeting there were actually two meetings going on. One was directly chaired and led by Hank, the other chaired and led by no one but taking place at the other end of the table. I commented to Hank afterwards that there was this separation, that it led to two meetings for at least some of the time, and certainly to a substantial failure among the group as a whole to interact. Thus, one of the reasons for the concerns he had expressed about the relative ineffectiveness of the group in 'getting together' or 'forming consensus' was that they simply were physically separate. I asked why this situation had arisen and why he let it continue.

He was bowled over by my observation, not because he had not noticed the physical situation, but because he had actually created it! 'Alan, I am a non-smoker and I can't stand people smoking near me. So I said they could smoke in meetings only if they sat well away from me.' We discussed alternatives to the problem, including the idea of providing explicit smoking breaks so that those who needed to could go out for a smoke rather than puffing it in his direction. The nature of the room and the table, however, meant that there would still be a considerable distance between him and the people furthest from him. I advised him that one significant contribution to resolving the problem of interaction between him and his subordinates would be to create a physical environment which removed him from the focal-point position, and which encouraged people to interact with each other. There was actually no way in which this could be achieved within his existing board room. It so happened, however, that we had been to a local hotel for another meeting, and the hotel had exactly what I had in mind—a round table!

The vice president booked the hotel room—and the round table—for his next meeting. With some help from me, he wrote a memo (writing memos instead of communicating orally was another of the issues) telling his subordinates of the new arrangements and why they had been set up. He also introduced a 'let's be kind to smokers' period. He even demonstrated the change of his behaviour in relation to that particular offer. Whereas previously it would have been his practice to make the decision for a break such as this, at the first meeting at the round table he said that he would respond rather to the needs of smokers. 'You tell me when you need a break.'

There was of course much more to this project, and much harder work to be done on the issues that Hank wanted to address. Again, it could be argued that too much attention was paid to the feedback and wisdom of an external facilitator. However, subsequent feedback from Hank and his colleagues confirmed that they had seen this physical change as a major contribution to their modestly improved effectiveness later.

This physical change is similar to one that occurred within project 2 in case 2 above. One of the major changes that occurred during that project was a reduction of digressions and interruptions. Before he was given feedback on what was actually happening, Herb allowed interruptions from any apparently important source—telephone calls, senior colleagues with a head round the door. The major improvement in this area, which was significant not so much in terms of the time wasted, but in terms of the frustrations experienced by his colleagues, was secured by the adoption and implementation of a simple rule: no interruptions except by Herb's boss, the group managing director. The other members of his team had followed his behaviour and had similarly allowed themselves to be interrupted during the meeting. In fact, once they had adopted a rule of no interruptions, Herb and his colleagues actually supported each other much more, with fortunately some helpful levels of humour in implementing the rule they had chosen for themselves.

I put these two decisions together at this stage because they gave me something I have never forgotten in subsequent interactions with directors, whether in a process mode or in an explicit learning mode. The turbulent emotions, frustrations and anxieties that grip many managers, and which are revealed in their behaviours in meetings, often represent a great need and challenge in terms of learning and development. Yet some of the most effective interventions I have made in these and subsequent cases have centred not on dramatic transformational requirements, but on much more prosaic issues. These have major advantages in terms of how obvious they can be to participants, even though it may have taken an outsider to point them out, and in terms of the relative ease of change behaviour.

In terms of organizational learning, these illustrations seem to me to carry an associated message. It is much easier to talk about fundamental change, about the desirability of transformational learning, than it is to achieve it. It is also all too easy to ignore some of the more modest contributions that can be made at a much lower level of ambition. Yet achievement at these lower levels may actually substantially determine achievement at higher levels. Would the American executives ever have been able to deal with some of their problems of interaction without the physical changes just described? Would the beliefs about the doubts about the seriousness of purpose of Herb ever have been resolved without the symbolism of the cut-off telephone?

CASE 1

As described in Chapter 1, the top team of this organization proceeded to a workshop the content of which primarily reflected concerns revealed in the diagnostic discussions and the subsequent review day. In that sense, it was a clear response to their expressed needs. In another sense, however, it expressed my values and beliefs as described in the Introduction to Part One.

At the design stage, I brought in a close colleague to share in both design and implementation of the proposed workshop. We proposed to the top management group, and they accepted, the following objectives:

1. To set aims, objectives and performance measurements for employee involvement (EI) and program management (PM)
2. To review and prepare plans for dealing with all major problems in EI and PM
3. To agree common language for EI and PM
4. To contribute to the design of next level workshops
5. To use participative processes to reach decisions throughout, including those reached on some 'normal' agenda items
6. To experience the value of explicit feedback

The first three of these were intended to address the issues raised in the original diagnosis and discussion. The fourth objective derived from the review discussion described in Chapter 1, where the proposal for next-level workshops had been put on ice. The remaining two objectives were not things that the top team had previously defined for themselves.

The process used for the workshop, held off-site over two days, was that the whole group was given a series of short inputs by one of us. After each input a task, for example definition of objectives for EI, was discussed in small groups. In these groups we acted as process consultants. In addition, during the two days the top team shifted into its normal method of operation on several ongoing agenda items. Discussion on these items was managed by Colin, the unit director, who used the processes that had been discussed before and during the workshop. At the end of each agenda item process feedback was offered, relating mainly to those issues covered during the workshop rather than additional (even though important) issues.

When the workshop participants set objectives and designed plans for dealing with employee involvement in program management, they were undertaking real management tasks required for the effective development of management in this unit. The decision to associate these tasks, which were real but none the less 'different', with discussion about familiar agenda items was much more risky than similar off-site workshops often allow. For example, this top team had to decide in the real time span of the workshop whether to allocate more time for a major discussion of a potential budget cut at the expense of workshop time on employee involvement issues. Issues about participative decision-making became central for everyone in this case.

Finally, decisions and action plans arising during the workshop were all taken back and put on the agenda for subsequent 'normal' management meetings. This design feature was important not only in terms of the principles we were trying to help managers to use, but also in helping them to avoid some of the reasons for failing to act on good intentions about participative management in the past. (It also shows a development of my understanding beyond the activity I had been involved with in case 2, project 2, described earlier in this chapter.)

As a result of the success of this workshop, I continued to work with Colin and his senior managers for a time, and also became involved in a major extension of the workshops to eventually hundreds of managers in the organization.

CASE 4

When we left case 4 in Chapter 2, the diagnostic workshop had led to a decision to proceed with the director development programme, following the feedback that John, the management development adviser, received from many of the participants. The chief executive, the most important individual to satisfy, had gone to the trouble of writing a most glowing letter about the process and my own credibility.

Chapter 13 describes the most recent version of a director development programme, since some aspects of it have changed and improved as I ran programmes after this case 4. There are, however, some important lessons drawn from this particular programme.

The first point is about the 'selling' of the programme. Participants had to be nominated by their individual companies, who paid a fee to the central management development department which was intended to generate the total cost for the programme. The role of John, the management development adviser, was crucial here in influencing everyone he could to provide nominations. This organization was not, nor were the individual companies, so desperate for director development that they were hammering on his door for places.

Despite the fact that this was being run for an international company, the participants in practice all came from the United Kingdom. This was explicitly accepted for the first programme, because the management development adviser thought it sensible in 'getting it off the ground'. On the second programme there were still no participants from outside Britain. The design of the programme can be seen as being partly responsible for this. On this first programme we ran six two-day workshops, at one-month intervals. Clearly, this was inconvenient for anyone who had to travel a significant distance. However, this scarcely applied to people from continental Europe. Even those who would be required to travel from the United States ought not to have been denied the opportunity—after all, it was by no means unknown for senior managers to come regularly to the United Kingdom for ordinary management meetings!

The fact was that the diagnostic process and the effective selling had been carried out with UK directors solely. The management development adviser really had nothing like the same influence outside the United Kingdom. We therefore finished up with a programme for an international company which, though it had participants with international experience, had no one actually currently located outside Britain. In terms of what was actually required within this business, this resulted in a significant lessening of impact. We made some attempt to reduce the problem by asking that the senior directors whom we involved in running a session at each workshop should be chosen from people with prolonged international experience, and this at least added to the international flavour.

This was one of a number of issues I would now describe as aspects of organizational learning which I recognized at the time separately without drawing them together. The following comments must first be placed in the context of the overall success of the programme. It was highly rated by the participants, by their organizational bosses and others involved in the programme and by the management development adviser. It met one of the primary criteria for sales success in that it led to repeat business, since a successor programme was run the following year.

Second, the comments are unbalanced in that they reflect not the successful characteristics of the programme, but rather the particular perspective of this book, which is about the extent to which my activities have helped to promote organizational learning. The honest answer in this case is 'Yes, but'. The 'but' is that more could have been achieved.

The first issue has already been mentioned—more genuine international participation. The second issue is one of participation within the organization on the nature of the programme, its development, progress and association with participants.

I proposed what was to this organization a unique arrangement: the setting up of a steering group, which would provide any clarification required on the content of the programme, would help secure nominations and stay in touch with participants, would review progress, give feedback to me as course director and, finally, would recommend decisions on a prospective second programme. I cannot see from my files whether these terms of reference were ever actually communicated to the steering group by the management development adviser, but certainly that is the way it operated. I was the only outside attender at steering group meetings.

The steering group was useful in several different ways. I collected my own notes on how things were going on the workshops, registering my own opinions, those of other tutors and feedback from participants. The presence of the steering group gave me the necessary reason for organizing these notes and presenting them in a way that not only kept them informed but, from my point of view very importantly, kept them aware that the programme was proceeding satisfactorily.

The steering group members were helpful because several of them took their own task very seriously and either saw their own nominees, or in one or two cases went out of their way to talk to other members of the programme. They also provided reassurance to me on the continuing relevance of the programme in the sense of relatively informal comments about what was happening within the organization. All of this helped, though at a fairly minimal level, in ensuring the continued organizational relevance of the programme.

By the end of the programme, I was feeling increasing frustration about the relative lack of involvement of John, the management development adviser. He had provided the original initiative, yet it seemed to me and to the programme participants that he was much less active than was desirable in attending the workshops, visiting participants and their bosses and generally identifying the programme as an important part of his work.

Directors as Counterparts

One area of interaction with the organization worked much more effectively. For each theme workshop, the steering group invited the chief executive of a major group of sub-

sidiaries within the organization to participate in the programme in two ways, as a counterpart to a tutor. First, he
would discuss with the tutor for the workshop the issues,
problems and questions that he felt should be addressed to
the workshop. Second, he would come along and take a $1\frac{1}{2}$
hour slot on the programme, in which he would talk about
current issues, problems and his own experience on the
subject under discussion, and respond to questions. All this
helped to make the programme much more genuinely
custom-tailored than is often the case with business school
programmes using familiar books and cases. The involvement
of these chief executives also made the participants feel that
the programme really was perceived as important by the
organization and not just by the participants and their
immediate sponsors.

Earlier I commented that I always propose that programmes and workshops are run on weekdays rather than
weekends, on the grounds that they are just another aspect of
real work. On this first programme, as a sort of compromise,
the client required that the workshops were run on Sunday
and Monday. The two-day length of workshop was deliberately chosen as that likely to be most convenient to senior-
level participants. In fact, the feedback from this programme
was that participants much preferred to have four-day workshops rather than what they saw as more frequent interruptions in their work schedule. They also vetoed Sundays for
future programmes.

I had constant detailed contact throughout the programme,
because I was present throughout. I was the lead tutor for two
of the workshops. For the other four my involvement varied.
On some I acted as a useful link by being able to refer to other
parts of the programme when relevant issues came up. It was
for example useful in the Strategy workshop to be able to refer
back to discussion we had had in the Job of a Director
workshop, and in the Team workshop. I worked closely with
the tutor to develop processes that focused not simply on the
pure team-role aspects, but on how these related to senior
executives carrying out their management work and their
projects as we had discussed them earlier in the programme.

In addition, my involvement centred on the last afternoon
of each workshop, which was devoted solely to a discussion
of individual projects, and on which I took the lead in
designing and facilitating the discussion. What I believe I
secured through this involvement (relatively luxurious and
expensive as it may seem to be) was a much greater degree of
integration between the subjects that were covered and issues

that developed during the programme, and a feeling of being able to suggest to tutors particular issues or priorities that were not necessarily susceptible to strategic planning in advance—even though this was set at a greater level, through their interaction with their 'counterparts', than I believe to be true on many such programmes.

I have already commented on the apparent success through repeat business. This was generated in part by the eagerness of programme participants to encourage others to come on the second programme. Their enthusiasm was especially significant. It is one thing from an organizational perspective for bosses to conclude that individuals have learned; and it is quite normal for individuals on a well designed programme to say that they have learned. However, for the individuals to be willing, as many of these were, actually to contact others to persuade them to come on the second programme was a significant contribution to the development of the second programme, and in some ways, therefore, to the development of organizational priorities for learning.

The views of the participants were captured in an extra session, not included in the original programme design, in which we reviewed the programme. The participants met myself and the management development adviser and went through the programme, making their suggestions on the level of success achieved through the different workshops. It was certainly a mistake of mine not to have built in such a review within the original project proposal—a mistake I have not repeated.

This programme contained two other areas which I have subsequently remedied. First, the process of learning to learn was not as successful as it could have been. I paid insufficient attention to structuring the sessions in which I asked them to review the learning they had acquired during the workshops, and the reviews of associated learning in between the workshops (see next chapter). The ways in which I now deal, as I see it more effectively, with this are described in Chapter 14.

My second major failure was that I did not provide for a major presentation of the projects undertaken by the participants. We had reviews during the programme, and the final programme review. We did not have a formal presentation of the projects and their results to clients and the steering group. This was a weakness because it meant that some of the participants finished the programme with really no formal review of their achievements (although it is fair to say that all of them had achieved quite a bit). It also missed a major opportunity to demonstrate to more senior executives what the projects were and what had been achieved through them, and in eliciting interest and further action from senior executives. In terms of generating organizational learning, this is a vital area through which individual learning can be extended into the reality of the managerial unit, and beyond that to larger organizational structures. In subsequent programmes, I have built in formal presentations.

6   What Sort of Achievements?

I first saw Shakespeare performed in the film *Hamlet* with
Laurence Olivier. A playgoer is supposed to have observed,
on having seen his first Shakespeare play, that it was full of
quotations. Memory tells me that I was particularly struck
with:

> But that the dread of something after death
> The undiscovered country from whose bourn
> No traveller returns,
> Puzzles the will
> And makes us rather bear those ills we have
> Than fly to others that we know not of?

I have always thought this a good description of the attitude
of quite a lot of managers towards management training and
development. What a genius Shakespeare was!

It has also increasingly seemed to me a relevant comment
about the *evaluation* of management training and development. Clearly, despite articles and books on the subject, the
number of management education or training courses subject
to serious evaluation rather than happiness sheets seems, on
both research and anecdotal evidence, to be very small.

If we turn to management development systems or
schemes, there is even less. One of the more naive periods of
my life was that which followed research that I carried out on
the development of directors. Very few organizations actually
had a clearly stated scheme for the development of directors
(even if they had one for managers). I found no case among 41
organizations, including some major UK multinationals, in
which they had attempted to evaluate what they claimed to
be trying to achieve.

I offered organizations that agreed to participate in the
research feedback on what had actually happened with the
directors I interviewed, within the bounds of individual

confidentiality. I gave this feedback to one of the participating organizations, which was in fact one of the very few that had set out a policy and drawn up a list of 'experiences', in terms of development activities that an individual was to have been involved in before being appointed to the main board. None of the four directors I interviewed had actually gone through all four of the 'experiences' set out in the policy: two had achieved three, and two had achieved two. When I gave the feedback, the personnel director implied, in that well-bred urbane way that is a peculiar property of some Englishmen, that I might possibly have missed some of the 'experiences' these individuals had been involved in. With equal courtesy, I replied that, since I was actually using his four required 'experiences' as a checklist, this was on the whole, with the greatest possible respect and with all the allowances for the fallibility of human memory, not the case. With further polite references to it being an interesting point to check, he went over to his filing cabinet and took (naturally from the top drawer) the personal files he had on the four directors. When he finished reading, he said that he had realized that there were some not wholly representative characteristics of the four individuals I had seen. Since the four directors had been chosen precisely because they *were* representative, I thought this slightly odd; but we moved on to less sensitive issues.

In the research report and subsequent book, I developed this kind of experience into the general proposition that most organizations did not know what they were trying to do in developing directors, and that those that had some idea had no process for evaluating it. I was so seized with the second of these two points that I proceeded to make it a major part of the talks I subsequently gave around the report and book. I took what I now see as the extraordinarily naive view that, if I highlighted for personnel directors and management development advisers a major weakness—the failure to check the success of their management development systems—they might be interested to recruit an experienced objective management development specialist like me to come and help them review their own systems. It shows how excitement about your own discoveries can blind you to the realities of the world in which we work. Since the publication of the original report, I have secured precisely one client who wanted an audit done on the effectiveness of his management development schemes.

I have thought about the implications of this. One possibility is that I have not marketed the idea successfully. Another is that the evaluation of development schemes is still not seen as a real issue by management development or personnel people. On my most cynical days (even rarer than the days on which I am naive), I think that I have been foolish to propose to personnel directors that the success of their efforts on management development should be audited—so long as they have apparently satisfied internal clients, why should they bother to collect data which, they might fear, would not just upset the apple cart but would say they should not be using apples at all?

What Do I Do about Evaluation?

The same concerns ought not to apply, however, to my own work. In my associated but differing roles as provider of a programme and learner, I must want to know how effective the programme has been.

Although my efforts have improved, I am not satisfied that I do enough on this. Perhaps I am another illustration of Chris Argyris's differentiation between 'espoused theory' and 'theory in use'. Argyris has shown that managers often claim to believe in a set of rules, concepts or theories, and indeed project them as the desirable way of behaving, yet in real situations behave quite differently. Not only do they behave differently, but, if asked, they show that they have relatively clearly worked out reasons for behaving that way.

My espoused theory in most of my books has certainly been in favour of the evaluation of management development. However, I have found that there are often particular circumstances in which such evaluation is not quite applicable. This chapter provides me with the opportunity to assess whether I have been operating at a higher level of hypocrisy, or whether there are distinguishable reasons relevant to the learning organization which explain some of the gaps.

I do not design and run knowledge-based sessions, which clearly are the easiest to evaluate. Nor is most of my work very strongly focused on skills or competences, which again can be assessed, although with much more difficulty. Also, I have become very wary of an approach that predicates objectives set by me or any one else for the individual learner. Statements like Mager's hierarchy of objectives, or anything else that is substantially prescriptive, take us into a teaching and training input process to which I have developed a strong antagonism. Since I do not work on programmes of qualification for managers, I am not faced with the quandary about fitting self-development, individual learning needs and learning style preferences into a programme that none the less 'covers the syllabus' and satisfies examiners or assessors through some process external to the learner.

I do not think I have used the word 'evaluation' with any of my clients in relation to a programme over the last 12 years. Instead, I talk about:

- Review
- Follow-up

CASE 1

The top-team workshop described was assessed at two levels. My co-tutor and I had carefully designed, proposed and got agreement to clear objectives as shown. He and I sat down afterwards and concluded the workshop had succeeded in terms of those objectives. The workshop was also a pilot in terms of process and some content for a proposed series of subsequent workshops. It was successful at that level also, since I was given the contract for carrying this process through. My notes of this time do not indicate why the client decided to go ahead, and whether he reviewed the success of the workshop in the structured form that my co-tutor and I did. The case illustrates one kind of evaluation: does the client want more? If he does at some level, then your process must have been successful. This is not a sufficient form of evaluation, in that it is not sophisticated, but it is practical from the point of view of both provider and receiver.

CASE 2

The fact of the second project in the organization described in case 2 was in itself a form of evaluation of the success of the first project, as the description in Chapter 1 shows. In fact, I did five different projects in that organization. They were all on the basis of 'Alan has been helpful on ...'. On two of the projects there was more serious evaluation than simply a feeling on the part of the participants that they had been helped.

Project 1 extended beyond the original report, and I became involved in actually helping participants to implement ideas on how to improve their effectiveness. There were two different measures of the success of the project. First, there was a major transformation in Sid's Monday management meetings. During my diagnostic phase with him, I had noticed both the ineffectiveness in terms of ideas contribution, and the inefficiency in terms of time spent on these meetings. One measurement was that managers did become more prepared to put up ideas. Another cruder, but very important, measure was that the meetings, which had originally lasted for a whole day every Monday, now lasted for only half a day.

I also engaged Sid and his managers in a review during the project of how far they thought managerial behaviour was changing, against the criteria they had set themselves. I was able to report, following a tour round Sid and his managers, that they all felt that things were going much better—and, indeed, I observed this at meetings. One of the errors of this process as I now see it is that I acted consistently not only as the data collector, but also as the sole informer. I had discussions with the managers, with Sid, and wrote a report on their views which they all saw; I discussed the report with Sid—but I never set up a meeting in which managers and Sid together discussed their achievements.

A more formal evaluation was built into project 2. At the beginning of the project, participants were asked to fill in a questionnaire assessing the effectiveness of these meetings—indeed, it was the consistent nature of the feedback that led to this stage of the project. The seven participants in the staff and divisional director were asked to assess the effectiveness of these meetings on a scale from 0 = strongly disagree to 3 = strongly agree. Among the results prior to the project being undertaken were:

> The objective of these meetings is clear to me:
> 0 (0)   1 (4)   2 (1)   3 (2)
>
> These meetings achieve worthwhile results:
> 0 (0)   1 (5)   2 (2)   3 (3)
>
> Meetings do not suffer unduly from digressions/
> interruptions:
> 0 (7)
>
> Issues important to me are resolved:
> 0 (1)   1 (4)   2 (2)
>
> These meetings show us working effectively as a team:
> 0 (4)   1 (3)

This original assessment of the effectiveness of management meetings, supplemented by the feedback presented to the participants, was designed to enable participants to focus on some of the causes of, and therefore potential remedies for, their dissatisfaction with the achievement being registered at the meetings.

In view of the comment I have made about the lack of

discussion, it is interesting to note that, in fact, behaviour in this group had shifted in the direction they all desired. For example, whereas four individuals had given a score of 1 on the clarity of objectives at the meetings, within two months no one gave this low a rating; there was a major shift from the judgement that meetings were frequently subject to digression and interruption; there was no significant shift on the question of importance of issues and effectiveness as a team.

CASE 4

Here we move into a more traditional situation, with a defined programme for development. The review process I initiated covered the following stages:

1. Personal learning reviews during the workshops—'What Have I Learned So Far?'
2. Overall review by participants at midway stage
3. Steering group review at midway stage
4. Participant learning review day

My notes do not show whether a set of objectives for the programme was formally agreed. I did send out a note entitled 'the Nature of the Programme', which described the philosophy and process behind the programme as well as illustrating what was meant by 'themes' and 'projects'. What the subsequent review processes did was to focus on issues of personal learning, and of the effectiveness of the process, rather than on assessing achieved outputs.

Personal Learning Review

Each participant was asked in the first workshop to produce a mini personal development plan, and to keep a *learning log*. On each subsequent workshop each participant was asked to review his or her own progress against the personal development plan using the learning log. In addition, pauses for individual learning reviews were built into some but not all of the workshops. I show in case 5 below and in Chapters 14 and 15 how I have improved the process of personal learning review.

Participants' Mid-Programme Review

Time was set aside in the middle of the sequence of workshops for all the participants to review as a group and with me how successful the programme had been so far in meeting their needs, and what kind of additional help they needed to carry through the programme. The main benefit in learning process terms was that I had helped them identify more specific and concrete actions that they should have taken or could now take arising from the individual workshops.

One particularly interesting piece of feedback was that an individual who had been dissatisfied with one workshop proclaimed himself very satisfied indeed with a subsequent one. One of his colleagues, while agreeing with some of the flaws in the earlier workshop, pointed out that the nature of the subject, 'Strategy', lent itself to rather different impact and likelihood of immediate action compared with that of the second workshop, which was a structured approach to 'Team Management Roles'. This was a particularly valuable inter-action for me, because it reinforced a point I had actually built into the design of the Team Management workshop, in which we tried to focus some of the actions in terms of how different team role preferences would affect which people would do what kind of things in relation to Strategy.

Another piece of learning was the need to capture issues in writing and to ensure that these were circulated within the group of participants. I had previously taken a very relaxed view that they should note their own actions.

Steering Group

Meetings of the steering group generally focused on a formal report from me in writing on my perception of the level of success achieved through the workshop and any other issues arising. There was then general discussion from members of the steering group about the information they had acquired from participants. Generally the two sets of views coincided, but there were occasions when the strongly reported views of one or two individuals were perhaps overemphasized.

From the point of view of evaluation, the important role of the steering groups was not just to give immediate feedback but to encourage the view that assessing the impact of the programme was something that should be immediate and continuous rather than occurring at the end of the pro-gramme. This is clearer to me now than it was at the time.

Participant Learning Review Day

We spent an afternoon on this at the end of the programme, followed by a traditional end-of-course dinner attended by the group personnel director.

The participants were very clear that they did not want anyone else present during the actual review, including their management development adviser. They wanted it as a personal day which they would share with me as the course director. In practice, in the evening before and during the subsequent dinner they presented their views to the management development adviser and the personnel director. The objectives of the day were:

- For individuals to review, clarify and confirm the learning achieved through the workshops and projects
- For individuals to identify further steps for personal development
- To produce the basis for a formal review from the participants to the steering group, and other senior executives
- To produce examples of development and learning which could be used in promotional material within the company

The day confirmed what they had said previously—and on which, indeed the steering group had already acted—that the programme had been successful and that a further programme should be held in the following year. At the level of immediate customer satisfaction, then, the programme seemed to have been a success. However, there was no input from the bosses of the participants on the programme. This fault was remedied on the next programme, where the Learning Review 'Day' was turned into a full day including presentations on each project to the project client.

CASE 5

This programme differed from case 4 in that it was for a complete board rather than a collection of subsidiary company directors.

In this organization the objectives of the director development programme were set in advance as:

- To enable the board to develop its capacity for future change and growth
- To develop the capacity of individual directors to act in a corporate as well as a functional mode
- To assist the board in acting as an integrated team

There were three significant differences about the review processes employed, the first of which was that there was no need for a steering group representing a variety of different clients. Indeed, the measurement of success focused not only on a more coherent client group, but even more specifically on the views of the chief executive.

A second difference was in the origin of the programme, which was produced through the double-value process of personal development plans and analysis of group needs for the board, described in Chapters 2 and 4. Individuals arrived on the programme with their draft personal development plans, which would be used as the basis for reviewing progress both on these PDPs and on the issues emerging during the programme.

The third difference was that, instead of requiring individuals to conduct their own learning reviews about what they had gained during and at the end of each workshop, I asked them additionally to share these reviews with a colleague. By a fortunate chance there were odd numbers, so it was natural to pair the chief executive with me, which had a number of major advantages: it enabled him to be entirely open about his own needs; and it provided him with a chance to talk about issues he was observing during the programme, sometimes requiring feedback to himself and sometimes requiring comment about his own behaviour or that of his colleagues.

The pair reviews were much more successful than individual reviews had been on previous programmes. Individuals were paired by learning style differences, and this was found to be a very productive basis for exchange, as was shown in the feedback they were asked to give during a general session after the pair reviews.

A Learning Review Day was held, with a more detailed pre-questionnaire than that used in case 4. Participants looked back at content, methods, sequence, and also actions arising from the programme. Finally, they were asked to give an overall assessment of the programme against the three objectives set out above.

This review was held four months after the final workshop, which itself had been postponed three times. Up to the time of the final workshop, attendance and commitment had been remarkably good. Considering the problems faced by the board, the focus they managed, and the willingness of the chief executive in particular not to allow distractions during the workshops, were excellent. The delays in running the final workshop were frustrating to me, because I saw the commitment and momentum that had been generated in the previous four workshops slipping. (It is true that one postponement was due to the fact that the Queen was visiting the company on the days we had previously selected!)

Views about the effectiveness of the programme were predominantly favourable. Of nine participants, two expressed negative views. They are interesting for different reasons.

One participant, a Strong Activist, was the only participant to miss parts of the programme. His arrivals and departures became something of a running joke with his colleagues. As I found in drafting his personal development plan, he had little patience with courses; one of the high points of his experience had been when he left a time management course halfway through because of time pressures at work!

The second critical participant was in contrast a Strong Theorist, and had expressed dissatisfaction at the end of the first workshop on the grounds that not enough concepts had been presented to make him feel intellectually stretched. In subsequent workshops he actually participated fully and with apparent benefit, but at the final review he reverted to his view that he had not been fully satisfied.

During the Learning Review Day, I said that I felt the programme, although by all accounts and my own observation very successful overall, had failed in two areas. First, the board and individual members had taken on at each workshop a number of actions. Co-tutors and myself had from time to time advised them they were taking on too much and had helped them to prioritize their lists. However, even the reduced lists had in many cases not been successfully tackled. Although I gave details in support of this opinion, several of the board members were very unhappy at my comments and said that I was being unduly critical.

The other major area where I felt the programme was less successful than it should have been was on the achievement of participants' individual projects. Here I criticized myself more than them. I had failed to establish who was the client for the project—the chief executive or the board as a whole. Additionally, I should have recognized more quickly than I did that, because I chaired the project reviews at each workshop, they had become 'Alan Mumford projects'. I had attempted to get the chief executive to chair the reviews, but he produced what I saw as a smoke-screen about my independent objective style suiting the process better.

CASES 4 and 5: What was Missing?

The great problem in traditional training and education courses has been to assess whether participants actually apply in their real work what they have learned on the course. The action learning approach attempts to remove, or at least substantially to reduce, this problem by bringing real work into the course. Instead of confronting participants with the problem of transferring knowledge acquired about strategy to their development of strategy at work, the development of strategy takes place at the workshop. Instead of just talking about the principles of change, and going through some case studies, participants actually work on their current change issues—in this case changes in responsibilities, how to restructure part of the business, how to refocus the efforts of some functions. In one sense, therefore, the answer to questions on whether people were actually 'learning and applying' was felt by the participants and observed by me as course director. These were the issues we discussed in the final Learning Review Day.

However, the fact that some changes in knowledge, behaviour, effectiveness and interaction could be seen immediately on the programme with this real group does not at all resolve the issue of whether or to what extent participants carry through such changes subsequently. The missing element is any follow-up with the individuals themselves or with their bosses or colleagues to see how far changes are being carried through in ongoing managerial life.

There is an irony too in the fact that a programme designed around the integration of real work and learning encountered problems not in the acceptability of the principle to the participant, nor in the achievability of this within the design of the programme, but in the actual implementation of some of the real work developed through the programme.

The Value of Personal Development Plans

The first test of the value of personal development plans as described in Chapter 4 is whether the drafts I produce are accepted, first by the individual and then by the boss. In terms of acceptability, PDPs have proved themselves. These senior individuals generally comment that it is the first time they have had their development properly assessed. They also value the independence of an outside person to whom they can talk confidentially. Even more importantly, in terms of results, they see a much more careful analysis of themselves and of their development needs than they had previously thought to be possible, 'Because I have never really been asked to think seriously about this before'. Bosses similarly, in general, respond very favourably to what is presented to them. They are understandably less inclined to refer to the absence of previous analysis and discussion, and to focus more on the results of what has now been presented.

Interestingly, I very rarely get many compliments about the range and content of development solutions identified at the end of the PDP. This is the area in which I am certain I present a much wider range of possibilities with a sounder base than normal boss–subordinate discussions would provide. On the whole, participants pick up the ideas as useful and sometimes ingenious without giving quite the same emphatic exclamations of how they could not have achieved this on their own.

The next phase of assessment is whether the PDPs lead to an agreed plan of action. At their discussion, the individual and boss have a range of possible solutions in terms of development opportunities, from which they are expected to develop an action plan.

Even more important than whether individuals have actually produced an action plan is whether the action plan is put into effect. When I was an internal adviser I could follow through with the participants, check up with each party what had been agreed, what actions had been followed through and with what results. As an external adviser, I have not been in a position to do this in the relatively informal way I could before. My suggestions that I could take on such a role from outside have encountered resistance. In part, the resistance is that of the internal professional who really, and in a sense rightly, wants to turn the results of the PDPs back into the organization, with the manager and personnel director/management development adviser taking responsibility for following through on actions. This is the correct line to take. Unfortunately, I do not know whether the people who want to carry through this responsibility actually do so—in a few cases I suspect they do not. The other reason for my lack of subsequent involvement is that, inevitably, organizations see me as trying to sell my services for further work.

A Final Statement on Evaluation

The position of some of my clients on evaluation has been quite clear, and in terms of an action learning programme absolutely understandable. They see the benefits of the real work undertaken on the programme, the progress made on projects, issues tackled which had been unresolved probably for some time. From their point of view, particularly when there are clearly defined projects which have been achieved, evaluation is unnecessary. As a managing director said to me when I proposed a major evaluation programme, 'I can see why you want to do evaluation, because it is the professional and academically desirable thing to do. But I don't need it, because I already know how much money we have saved and made as a result of this programme.'

I am ambivalent about evaluation in its largest sense. I would be delighted to find a client who was really prepared to engage in a major evaluation activity. Writing this chapter has reminded me that I ought to be more courageous in proposing more rigorous evaluation to more clients. My ambivalence arises because if they are not keen on it—which means especially that they are not willing to pay the money for it to be done—I am not likely to want to put a lot of time and effort into trying to change their minds.

Follow-Up

The area in which I feel more determined is that of follow-up.

In case 7, I did sit down (without charging a fee) about ten months after the workshop to review both it and personal development plans with my client director, Tony. There was quite a lot of good news about follow-through and implementation.

Tony looks at the actions set out in the PDPs at his normal quarterly management review with each individual. He conducts a review after each group management meeting, based on going round the task cycle and learning cycle. The subgroup working on 'world class' had achieved quite a lot—but he made a note to check what they had learned. He has invented an award which he calls 'Stolen with Pride'. This picked up a point made in several PDPs about ways of learning from people outside one's own division. He now asks at each group management meeting who has taken up an idea from someone else, and awards points for it.

I ought to take a much more assertive line in building in additional days after the programme or after personal development plans, in which I could meet individuals and discuss with them what they have actually done. I will be proposing this as 'There is life beyond the Learning Review Day'.

7   What Does This Mean for the Learning Organization?

None of the cases covered so far were requested or offered by me as organizational learning. I turn later in this chapter to some general considerations about the origins and meaning of organizational learning, but I start by reviewing these experiences against my own definition of the term:

> The learning organization is one that creates an environment where the behaviours and practices involved in continuous development are actively encouraged.

One way of understanding what is being attempted and what may be achieved in a learning organization is given in Fig. 7.1. This describes four areas of focus for managerial learning at work, which are also hierarchical levels.

- The learning organization
- Work-groups
- One-to-one relationships (e.g. to boss or mentor)
- Individual learners

Figure 7.1   Focus for managerial learning

One of the problems I have with much of the literature on organizational learning is that it does not provide effectively for learning at these different levels. Too often, there is an assumption that you leap from being effective individual learners (with no clear view of how this is achieved) to becoming a learning organization on a grand, not to say apocalyptic, scale. The cases show a gradual change in my work towards a more effective integration of the lower three levels. This chapter reviews the extent to which the *behaviours and practices* used in the development and implementation of these programmes illustrates, and provides the basis for, *continuous development* beyond the programme.

Diagnosis

My work has been undertaken primarily in order to meet the needs of the business organization. There is a different proposition, which sustains the idea of self-development, or general education or training with no specific organizational purpose. Either of these can in practice facilitate some part of the necessary development of individuals or groups required for organizational purposes. However, the cases reviewed here were required, designed and implemented to meet organizational purposes.

Does a learning organisation encourage any kind of learning activity, however remote from immediate or longer-term organizational goals, simply on the grounds that 'learning is a good thing', that any kind of learning promotes good habits about learning, or that it is the right of individuals to pursue self-actualization? I can see these as legitimate objectives in certain circumstances; however, they do not fit my experience or definition.

Shared Commitment

To an increasing degree, participants in the cases described here were invited to commit to the decision that the process should be undertaken. This was often an uncomfortable period for me in terms of frustration, worry and extended time-scales, but it is likely to be the best decision-making process for the encouragement of the kind of activities through which I want to offer help.

Participants also were asked to respond to a particular kind of process. They were asked to commit to their own definition of their own development needs, both at an individual and at a group level. They were asked to commit to a process—action learning—which offered greater opportunities, but also greater risks, than many other forms of management training or education. They were asked to commit to an integration between real work problems and activities and the explicit intervention of development-focused work.

The Seductiveness and Terror of Real Work

Cases 2 and 8 describe the most intimate interventions I have made in the real-work situation. Immediacy of need, and the equal opportunity to provide help increasingly at the moment of need, made for very powerful and influential interventions. Other cases with explicit developmental objectives sustained a similar but more distant emphasis on real work—and often carried the risk of desirable actions later being overwhelmed by the clangorous demands of day-to-day priorities. I suspect now that I have accepted too readily that people will not act as they plan to because my own managerial experience shows me what terribly conflicting lives they lead.

Professor John Morris once illuminated for me the place of simulation in managerial learning. He argued that it was the relative unreality contained within simulations that enabled people to focus on the process rather than the task. I have grown increasingly to dislike simulations. Yet I have not fully resolved the problem of how to enable managers to make the best use of real work for development purposes.

Explicit Learning Cases 2 and 8 are at the extremes of intervention, focused on issues of immediate managerial effectiveness rather than development. In neither case did I raise issues about what the clients were learning, as distinct from what they were being facilitated or enabled to do. In other cases not quoted in this book, I have made a similar focus on effectiveness rather than development needs. Working as a sounding board for a managing director or defining terms of reference for a board have not really been about the behaviours and practices of continuous development.

These experiences, however, have sharpened my view that, for the learning organization construct to be meaningful, learning has to be up front as an issue. The encouragement of effective management practices can lead to the creation of a more effective organization—without necessarily leading to the creation of a learning organization.

However, those cases reviewed here in which learning has been an explicit objective and process do fall within my definition of a learning organization. Where the process (the task cycle, the learning cycle) is proposed, reviewed, discussed and constantly referred to in the programme or in the personal development plans, then I have assisted in embedding appropriate behaviours and practices. When I have discussed learning style preferences and their significance for learning on a programme or, similarly, the crucial features of preferred choices within a personal development plan, I have contributed to the learning organization. The contribution was, however, primarily at the lower three levels of Fig. 7.1.

The most recent of my developments has been to provide a better basis for improved one-to-one relationships. One of the best results from a workshop I ran for directors (see case 7) was when the group decided to take up the process on its own account and follow through with their subordinates, not just in relation to the particular interrelationships on which the workshop had focused, but in proposing to their subordinates that they should go through the same PDP process on which they had worked with me—without my intervention. That does represent progress in terms of expanding appropriate behaviours and practices beyond those with whom I have had my immediate enlivening effect.

Continuous Development

I felt least happy about the absence of information on the extent to which, as a result of my efforts, individuals have continued their development after their involvement with me. My comments in Chapter 6 about evaluation and follow-up apply here.

Incremental or Transformational Learning?

One of the major differences between my definition of organizational learning and other definitions (see page 88–89) is that on the whole I have always seen my efforts as towards incremental rather than transformational learning. Again, there can be differences of definition here, but I take the view that largely I am building from existing experience and existing levels of understanding. I am enabling people to understand and better use their current knowledge derived from past experience, now tested against some new propositions and new demands. The incremental changes that have been achieved could in some senses, and by some people, be described as being of such a size and nature that it really has represented a transformation. However, I have a distaste for the idea of transformation. I think it unrealistic and therefore unachievable in most circumstances. Requiring individuals to think about running before they have walked may mean that they will fall over. This analogy seems particularly appropriate because, unless people have fully understood and worked through their understanding of their current experiences, needs and requirements, I do not think they can grapple with the larger, more problematic, more emotional issues involved in transformation.

An example can be seen in case 2. The participant managers in project 1 told me that 'the director will never change'. They believed that his behavioural characteristics were fixed, and they lacked any experience of seeing him change; they were quite sure that nothing of significance would happen. In fact, he did make major changes in his own behaviour, with consequences for the behaviour of his management group as a whole. Was the fact that he learned how to run his weekly management meeting in half the time an incremental piece of learning or a transformational one? I would define it as incremental, because it built on some skills he already had but was under-utilizing. Yet, some of his managers saw it as a transformation.

Building Back into Reality

The learning organization is not the one that provides the most courses, the most formal planned development, the best learning resources. It is the organization that provides the most effective learning in and around the reality of work. This is difficult—other priorities get in the way. Reviewing these cases has shown me that it is necessary to take even more steps than I was taking to ensure integration of effort. Actions decided on during the programme must be pushed out from the programme and back on to the plans and agendas of managers in their normal situations. Case 1 provides an excellent example. Workshop decisions were placed on the normal top-team management meeting agenda. My efforts on other occasions to ensure that similar things happen with strategic plans or decisions about priorities have not been as successful as is necessary if the full integration effort between 'development' and 'normal organizational working' is to be achieved.

Learning Reviews and Continuity

The emotional and practical tug of 'real work' is always likely to overwhelm reflection about process in any form. Pressures of getting through more in a day are always likely to gobble up time that ought to be devoted to reviewing what has been achieved so far. Just as in normal work managers are reluctant to give enough time to review and discuss process—how things are being done—so they are surprised to be set a task of reviewing the learning they have achieved at ten past three on day 1 of a director programme. In some early versions of director programmes I was too low-key, insufficiently pressing about the purpose, need and results of learning reviews. I would explain the purpose, set them the task of doing the learning review orally, and then resume the rest of the workshop 20 minutes later. I was in a quandary— knowing they would benefit from this, and yet seeming to make a fuss about an issue that was of prime concern to me, rather than to them.

Now I emphasize the objectives, set them a clear task in writing and ask them to share the results of the learning review. This is a crucial way of reinforcing the behaviours and practices that they need to carry away from the programme if they are to become involved in continuous development.

Personal Demonstration

I always tell participants on my programmes that I keep notes on what is going on. When they do their learning reviews, I tell them that I am doing the learning review as well. I have rarely had anyone ask me to share my learning review. I would not volunteer to do so because I think this would place my learning in a position of greater significance than is desirable. But the fact that I am doing what I am asking them to do is important to place in front of them.

In addition, I consistently go over with them the design of the programme. I explain at the beginning of the programme the concepts of the learning cycle and the task cycle—and these we refer back to during the programme. Participants are asked to analyse and assess what we have done so far. Where have we been on the cycle? Where are we now?

Defining the Learning Organization

During the Second World War there was a popular UK radio programme, 'The Brains Trust'. The four participants responded to questions put to them on issues of the day (not political, because for many years BBC programmes were not allowed to discuss issues of current political significance). One of the regular members was C. E. M. Joad, a philosopher of populist rather than academic bent. He became very well known for his frequent response to questions, 'It all depends what you mean by ...'

This chapter reviews the extent to which the activities described in previous chapters contribute either:

• To the understanding of a learning organization

or

• To the effective practice within a learning organization

In terms of my own definition:

> The learning organization is one that creates an environment where the behaviours and practices involved in continuous development are actively encouraged.

This definition differs significantly from those offered by other conceptualizers of organizational learning—e.g. Argyris, Senge, Pedler, Boydell and Burgoyne. For the purposes of this book, I do not need to go into a detailed contextual analysis of the differences. I simply state two of these definitions below because it may facilitate an understanding of my own definition:

Peter Senge
Organisations where people continually expand their capacity to create the results they desire, where new and expansive patterns of thinking are nurtured, where collective aspiration is set free, and where people are continually learning how to learn together.

Mike Pedler, John Burgoyne, Tom Boydell
An organisation which facilitates the learning of all its members and continually transforms itself.

One of the virtues of my own definition is that it encourages people to look at the issues, which seems to me to be most fundamental, given that my own interests are better expressed by the term 'behaviours and practices' than in the no doubt more exciting possibilities of 'transforms itself' or 'collective aspiration'. I am simply not personally comfortable with these grander, more visionary concepts. Naturally, I provide another, less self-centred justification. When I have tested the Senge and Pedler definitions on directors and senior managers, although a few have found the concepts illuminating and stimulating, more have expressed puzzlement—'What is actually meant by...?' Of course, one of the values of a definition is precisely that it can cause people to worry, to debate, to argue and finally to tease out meaning, a process that can be stretching and useful. However, I find that most managers are impatient with this relatively luxurious approach. Since I share their impatience to a significant degree, I prefer my much more prosaic earthbound definition.

Is the Learning Organization Really So Different?

The length of experience I now have in management development provides a number of benefits, including that of perspective. Major solutions to management development over 30 years have included:

- The fundamental requirement for interpersonal sensitivity—T-groups
- Managerial styles, managerial grids
- Management by objectives
- The Harvard Case Method as the uniquely realistic approach to management education
- The creation of business schools as centres of excellence
- Self-development
- Organization development

- Action learning
- Outdoor training

So, when 'The Learning Organization' appears on the management development conspectus as the uniquely appropriate destination for effective development at all levels, I feel a sense of *déjà vu*, a phrase that accurately conveys a certain touch of French world-weary cynicism about a new venture. The tendency to cynicism is compounded when authors claiming to follow the otherwise admirable lead given by Senge and Pedler proceed to write articles claiming either that they already work in a learning organization, or that they have made significant steps towards finding this Holy Grail. The original innovative authors are by no means to be blamed for people writing articles which five or ten years earlier would probably have claimed to be centred on an action learning approach to management development or organization development. In the same way that people wrote articles about a small and perhaps useful piece of process consultancy and called it 'organizational development', so subsequently have we seen articles proclaiming the 'virtues' of action learning, which in practice have merely rediscovered the virtues of tacking on a project to the end of a course or MBA.

Am I Making Larger Claims?

So far I have been asked by only one company to help it develop some ideas on its capacity as a learning organization. I smile when I recollect what happened. The chief executive of the company had picked up from somewhere—perhaps from his involvement in some high-powered management education committees—the view that you could be an effective company only if you were a learning organization. He issued a pronouncement that the company was to take the action necessary to turn itself into a learning organization (without, I later discovered, any substantial discussion with anyone else in the company).

The personnel director decided to gather his senior personnel colleagues from headquarters and the operating divisions to discuss how this pronouncement was to be put into effect. He and his senior colleagues were delighted that their chief executive had taken such an innovative step, which they were sure would enable them to get a number of things done which would otherwise be more difficult. They invited me to join in a workshop which would discuss the issues involved in becoming a learning organization. It seemed to me that one of the most important questions was where they currently stood—how far along the path towards being a learning organization did they see themselves as being? For this purpose I proposed that we used my Learning Diagnostic Questionnaire (see Chapter 10), which set out the behaviours and practices I thought to be involved. My client rejected the use of my own or any other instrument in the group that would be meeting for the workshop. 'I am rather worried about what the results might show.' 'We really need to discuss the principles rather than looking at hard data at this stage.' 'It is much too dangerous at this stage for us to see conflicting results from different divisions.'

I mentioned these 'bandwagon' articles, and this last experience, because I have a real concern that sticking a label on an old product, or refusing to take up the significant new challenges offered by organizational learning, will bring the excellent, innovative, large-scale ideas into disrepute.

What Does Learning Mean?

The next issue of definition is what I mean by the word 'learning'.

> Learning has happened when people can demonstrate that they know something they did not know before (insights and realizations as well as facts), and/or when they can do something they could not do before (skills).

That is it—no more discussion?

Learning is both a process and an achievement—as well as a journey. The crucial point is that it is primarily about outputs, and therefore gets us away from the horrors of training and education inputs. I do not find it helpful to distinguish between learning and development—and it is interesting to note that we are talking about something called the *learning* organization, not the *developing* organization. Interesting, and also paradoxical, because in many ways the definitions of learning by Senge and Pedler fit better what Mike Pedler and Tom Boydell in *Managing Yourself* (Fontana, 1985) tried to distinguish as development rather than from learning.

PART TWO

MODELS, THEORIES AND DIAGNOSTIC INSTRUMENTS

Sid, the client in case 2, project 1, had a mannerism which forecast that he was going to say something that pleased him a great deal. He put his thumbs in the waistband of his trousers and moved them sideways very quickly several times. Then would come his pronouncement—the condemnation of someone's idiocy, a discovery of some interconnection which explained a problem, a merciless analysis of the defects in a letter to which he was replying.

One of his pronouncements was, 'You know that Hermann Goering said that whenever he heard the word "culture" he reached for his revolver. I reach for mine whenever I hear the word "theory".'

I struggle over abstract concepts, high-level theories, complicated models (see Chapter 17). I do not think that the content of the chapters in Part Two would cause Sid actually to reach for his revolver. They set out further arguments, and the practical processes required, to support my claim that organizational learning depends on explicit learning processes.

Part One has taken readers round the learning cycle:

- My experiences
- My review and reflection on those experiences
- The conclusions I have drawn
- Some plans for future action by myself

Part Two provides a similar learning cycle. However, it offers a more substantial element of explanation—of the conclusions I have drawn from my own experience, and from my examination of the conclusions, or theories, or generalizations, offered by others.

The interest, temptation and satisfaction involved in producing a new theory or model has not greatly informed my work. This is indeed a characteristically British understatement.

I have only once attempted a major model (see pages 104–106), and then an academic colleague told me that it was a typology and not a model. I was so pleased at having produced a model at all that I was not in fact hurt by this comment.

All of which is to say that I see myself as having operated essentially at a level of improved practice based on sensible generalizations, rather than on high-level theoretical constructs. I have often been told that this is one of the reasons why people like my books, and my direct work with them. Of course, I am delighted to believe that this is true—but I wish I were also better at constructing or valuing theories. It is a weakness that limits some areas of learning for me—and also what I offer to others.

8 How Organizations Learn from Work

CASE 1

CASE 1

The organization reviewed in Chapter 1, case 1, was responsible for the design of new products. The design process and associated management efforts followed the following sequence:

1. Data were collected on the successful and unsuccessful elements in previous products, and on customer desires for the new product.
2. A design specification was drawn up.
3. The design was tested through a pilot product.
4. The behaviour of the product in the test was analysed.
5. The product was amended or redesigned (if necessary).

The company had begun to experience a loss of market share, partly attributable to higher design costs compared with competitors. Before I became involved with them, they had been through another process:

1. They received data on the greater productivity of competitors.
2. They reviewed the data to try and establish the causes of the greater productivity.
3. They reached a conclusion about the main causes, which led to their decisions on a slimmed-down management structure and a changed requirement in managerial behaviour.
4. They planned what to do as a result of their conclusions (leading eventually to the entry of Alan Mumford, as described in Chapter 1).

CASE 2

This organization was involved in a production process. The product had been newly designed, and there were problems of interaction between departments working on different parts of the product. The work involved, and the management process through which it was controlled, followed a familiar pattern:

1. A plan was drawn up.
2. The plan was implemented.
3. Problems and/or difficulties emerged, requiring analysis and explanation.
4. Regular reviews were held of progress.
5. Consistent failures to achieve the plan led to an insistence on more reviews, with more data.
6. New plans were produced as a result of the reviews.

CASE 6

This organization had an established selection process for managers, which gave special emphasis to the results of psychological assessment. The company was seen to move from a successful to a much less successful position, and as a result appointed a new chief executive. He asked for a report on why managers, who had been appointed through a diligent and apparently previously successful selection process, were now themselves having to be removed. (He excluded only two senior managers from this assessment—himself and his predecessor.)

As his adviser, I presented him with a report which:

- Gave him the data (how many managers had been appointed, the frequency of turnover, the level of success or failure)
- Reviewed the changed environment—managers who had apparently been successful in companies that were growing were found to be unsuccessful during a recession when the requirements for their performance changed.
- Concluded that there were three reasons for the failure of the selection process:

    (a) Lack of attention to detail in personnel specifications
    (b) Underemphasis of the actual achievement of managers (especially on internal promotion) as compared with their supposed potential
    (c) Overemphasis of the supposedly scientific and objective psychological assessments, evidence from which was often taken as more important than any other element in the selection decision

All the above cases demonstrate a process that operates consistently in management. The same phenomenon is true for the daily smaller-scale operations in which managers struggle to remain afloat in a sea of troubles, e.g.:

* Why has that machine broken down?
* John is ill today: what can we do to replace him?
* Suzy is threatening to leave unless we give her different work.

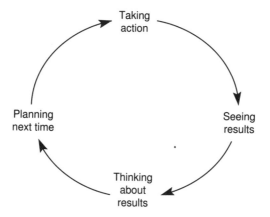

Figure 8.1 The task cycle
Source: P. Honey and A. Mumford, *Manual of Learning Opportunities*, Honey, 1989

On workshops, I produce during discussion, or show on the overhead projector, the task cycle (Fig. 8.1). Sometimes of course people think that 'Planning' ought to be the first step. So we have some discussion perhaps about what 'ought' means, and if necessary I point out that plans are never actually the first step—they have always been preceded by experiences, data and decisions about what to do as a result of the data. Those decisions then lead to planning.

Of course, this has the neatness and regularity appropriate for a model. However, unless they have been on decision-making courses, managers are very rarely aware of such a sequence, nor do they operate in neat stages or steps. But as a simple model, the task cycle is something they recognize and would believe that they adhere to, even though in practice they quite often leap from an event taking place to a plan for action, with little time spent on collecting data and clarifying conclusions from the data.

What Do these Cases Demonstrate?

The cases described above all show management in action to try to improve performance—management thinking its way through to improvement by recognizing a problem or an opportunity, collecting data about it, reaching a conclusion or a decision, and then planning what to do next.

In a sense, therefore, all these cases demonstrate an organization in the process of learning. The managers acquired new experiences or better understanding of existing experiences; they collected data or, as they more often put it, knowledge about what was going on; they thought about the data, tried to fit it into their larger understanding of their world, and reached decisions about it; finally, they drew up plans of action resulting from these thinking activities.

Yet, by the definition I am using, these organizations were not learning organizations, because the learning process and the consequences of the process were not identified, either in advance or afterwards, as learning processes or consequences. If faced with this fact, the managers might well have argued that it did not matter. They would have been most likely to say that what is important in management is the ability to undertake action, not whether you can fully articulate the processes by which you decide on the action. They would argue further that, since those actions depend on processes of review and reflection and conclusion, they are really engaged in learning although not consciously using that expression.

The contention of this book is that is *does* matter, because, without the overt identification of what has been learned, major learning opportunities of two different kinds will have been missed. The first is an understanding that the sequence of events, and the kind of thinking going into the problem-solving process mentioned here, contain wider possibilities. If learning can be identified as an aspect of the process, it can then be recognized as something natural, realistic, frequent—not something delivered in a package called 'training', 'education' or even 'learning'. The significance of this point is that it then becomes possible to encourage managers to recognize and make use of more opportunities for learning from real work experiences. In addition, it becomes feasible to suggest that they engage in some closer examination of the possibility of generalizing from particular experiences—which, as we will see later, is one of the defining characteristics of effective learning.

The second reason for trying to improve managers' recognition of these experiences as learning as well as task experiences is that we can respond to the often hazy beliefs ('theories') about learning from experience, while at the same time improving their understanding of the learning process involved. The question of what managers mean by 'learning from experience' is developed further in Chapter 9. My research with directors showed that even those who had taken part in significant off-the-job training or educational experiences frequently identified on-the-job experiences as more fundamental to their learning. The familiar clichés of 'learning from experience' or 'learning the hard way' rolled off the tongues of directors just as they have done for most managers I have met over the years.

What managers mean by such phrases is often something on a smaller scale than the major situations, projects and problems mentioned earlier in the cases quoted. They do learn from significantly new projects—but they also learn from more regular tasks or routines. They learn from being placed in new situations—but sometimes they learn from new participants in old situations. They learn from difficulties and sometimes from failures—they learn something, but often not enough, from success. They will frequently say, until they are asked to delve more deeply, that they simply learn from what worked and what didn't, either for themselves or from observing others in action.

Essentially, managers are focused on their work experiences because they are primarily people dedicated to task achievement. They are planners, reflectors and conceptualizers only to the extent to which they believe this to be necessary to achieve their task. Individuals who seem over-endowed with either a capacity in or a preference for any of these three processes will normally be called an 'intellectual', with the proviso, sometimes spoken and sometimes unspoken, that an intellectual is thereby disabled from being an effective manager. Managers learn from doing tasks, resolving problems and seeing the consequences of decisions, in the same way that the 'organizations' described in the above cases in some sense learned in order to change their processes, and learned from the changes they made.

The crucial point is that, if we can enable managers to see that they do not have to switch themselves away from real-work activities in order to learn, or to make major changes in their preferred sequence of thinking, we will have made a major contribution to embedding learning in organizational practices.

Of course, learning from your own experience, or from observation of the experience of others, within your own organization may be an entirely insufficient response to the actual needs. Indeed, it was from the recognition that, in the light of changing recognition of the purposes of management and of the skills needed to read those purposes, that the process we now call management development began.

From Teaching to Learning through Task

Serious effort on the structured formal development of managerial skills began in the United States before the Second World War, but effectively came to be taken up in Britain only after the war. It has gone through various changes of technique and understanding.

Management as a Taught Process

There still sits elegantly on the green banks of the Thames, 'Henley, the Management College'. I first encountered it as 'The Administrative Staff College'. Outside the formal management education structure, as it then was, it offered a 40-week course representing the confluence of two British traditions. The first was the tradition of the skilled amateur, who carried through professional duties in a non-confrontational style associated with the belief that successful managers were a generic breed—if you could manage one kind of organization, you could manage another. The original version of Henley existed at the time when it was absolutely natural to have ex-generals running the newly nationalized British Rail and the long nationalized British Broadcasting Corporation.

The second of these British traditions affecting Henley management courses in the 1950s and 1960s was a belief that management, because it was such a generalizable activity, could best be learned by a gentlemanly exchange of opinions. Henley organized its work around syndicates—collections of managers who were given subjects to discuss, the results of whose endeavours were presented to urbane college staff. Their beliefs formed their process, because beliefs about generalizability led to a process that encouraged generalization.

This syndicate process stood in explicit opposition to the favoured management education process in the United States, the Harvard case study method. The hard edge of the case study method was rejected by Henley and its followers on two grounds, one explicit, the other implicit. The explicit ground was that building management learning through the analysis of 50, 100 or 150 cases which dealt with specific circumstances was both tediously detailed and hideously inappropriate, since what was needed was the capacity to generalize. The implicit, usually unacknowledged, reason was: 'moreover, the American approach to business is not really ours'. Since then as now the United Kingdom was demonstrably both less efficient and less effective than the United States (a phrase from the US guru Peter Drucker), it took only 20 years for the United Kingdom to change its approach to management learning.

Suddenly, with the Franks Report in 1963, management education in a university setting was to provide the answer; moreover, it was to do so through business schools modelled on US experience—i.e. that management could be taught provided you had properly equipped teachers. (Henley prided itself on not having teachers—thus, the delightful coincidence of syndicates which could be helped along a bit, rather than classes which needed to be taught.)

Belief in the virtues of the tough-minded American business school approach was however modified by a deep-seated British characteristic. If the new business schools were to opt for the predominant American method, they would choose the case study as the prime vehicle. But the British have learned over hundreds of years of history that strong beliefs, direct and firm attachments to any particular cause, any vital statement of political or religious belief, can lead to revolution and war. Thus, the new business schools prided themselves in being catholic in their selection of methods.

In my early days in management development, I used the syndicate approach in the most senior course I ran, largely following the pattern of those who had originally established the course. But I introduced case studies because I thought they demanded a tougher mental discipline, and because I thought people would be stimulated by specific illustrations of management problems.

Along the way, I was also touched by, and recoiled in horror from, another great American contribution—T-groups. Initially sceptical about the idea of groups that got together to discuss group members' relationships with one another away from the work setting, with no tutorial input, I gradually turned from scepticism to outright disbelief. This was caused partly by personal experiences in which the T-group approach was used. Also, I had read the literature and met a few individuals who had been through the process. Some of them seemed to be like shell-shocked soldiers returning from rat-infested trenches in the First World War.

However, in a later derivation of the T-group, i.e. the Organization Development Movement, and especially in the work of Ed Schein, the ideas behind the phenomenon of process consultancy when applied in the work context to task-related issues did have a profound impact on me. Hence the kind of work I attempted in case 2.

Self-development and Management by Objectives

I became increasingly convinced that management development was more horticultural than mechanical. It was much more about providing an environment in which individuals could grow than it was about constructing managers from metal. The extraordinary idea that you could not *force* anyone to learn, but could encourage them to do so if you provided the right nutrients, seized me, and took me into the philosophy and detailed approach of self-development, on which I was one of the early UK authors.

Increasingly, I saw that the so-called transfer problem arising from management education and training was inevitable, given the substantially unreal content of even good courses.

Management by objectives was fundamental also because it took me away from generalized training solutions, just as the self-development approach did, towards the specifics of what individuals were trying to achieve. Oddly, for a long time I managed to operate with different people in quite different ways, working on Management by Objectives with some managers and on Learning and Development Processes with others, and never quite drawing them together (hence, again, case 2).

Putting Action and Learning Together

I read two of Reg Revan's books in the 1960s and some papers passed on to me by one of our directors who had been impressed when he had heard him in a conference. The thrust, however, as I recall it was all towards scientific management in one guise or another, and towards statements about management of systems. It was not until I heard Reg at an IPM conference after his major experience in Belgium that I really encountered his unique and, as I believe, earth-shattering contribution to management development. I was initially much impressed by the paper he delivered on this theme, and then I fear enjoyed even more his demolition of a respected IPM vice president who had the temerity to question the scientific basis of his conclusions. His ideas on action learning finally caused me to bring together my two areas of work. Since I was so seized with the idea of working with managers directly on how they should be effective, and had also, through the personal development plan approach, taken up the idea of development fundamentally centred around job experiences, action learning provided two-thirds of the integration I needed.

Action Learning

My version of the essential elements of action learning is as follows:

- Learning for managers should mean learning to take effective action. Acquiring information and becoming more capable in diagnosis or analysis has been overvalued in management learning.
- Taking effective action necessarily involves actually *taking* action, not recommending action or undertaking an analysis of someone else's problems.
- The best form of action for learning is work on a defined project or an ongoing problem which is significant to the managers themselves. Either project or problem should involve implementation as well as analysis and recommendation of action.
- While the managers should have responsibility for their own achievements on their own project, the learning process is a social one; managers learn best with and from each other.
- The social process is achieved and managed through regular meetings of managers to discuss their individual problems or projects. The group is normally called, in action learning terms, a 'set'. The managers, originally called 'comrades in adversity' by Revans, are perhaps better described as 'comrades in opportunity'.
- Finally, the role of the person providing help for members of the set is essentially and crucially different from that of the normal management teacher: here, the role is not to teach (whether through lecture, case or simulation), but to help managers learn from exposure to problems and to each other. As Revans says, action learning attacks 'the inveterate hankering of the teacher to be the centre of attention'.

This process is more than a rephrasing of learning from experience. Crucially, the idea of people working together in a set to discuss a defined problem or project differs from two other apparently similar types of learning from experience. It differs in structure and intention, and certainly in results, from the informal though natural exchange of ideas and wisdom which occurs in any management team discussing any management problem. It also differs from group discussions which occur on management training, where, even if real problems are discussed, they are discussed only because the programme exists, not because the problems have brought about the programme. Even more fundamentally, action learning differs from experiential processes such as business games, outdoor training and Lego bridge-building, which focus on process through simulation, not on task and process through reality.

Action learning asks managers to focus primarily on their own-life experiences rather than dissecting bodies such as case studies of how other managers have behaved in other situations. It differs too in providing for the delivery of recommendations for action which are centred on the ongoing reality of their organizations, not on the different, because simulated, reality of a course context.

Cases 4, 5 and 7 in this book were explicitly designed according to this philosophy and methodology.

Finally, Kolb and Knowles

I discovered David Kolb's work on *The Learning Cycle and Individual Learning Styles* in 1975. I later discovered Lewin's aphorism that 'there is nothing so practical as a good theory'. Kolb's theory I found marvellously illustrative of some major reasons why people did not learn effectively. The learning cycle showed inefficiencies of design, especially in off-the-job courses, but also in the provision of a method for learning on the job. The learning styles proposition, which of course is Kolb's unique discovery (whereas the learning cycle has several fathers), was even more mind-blowing—and eventually led to my work with Peter Honey on our own version of learning styles.

Bringing the Stages Together

If I had been more interested in theories and models, I would have brought these stages of understanding and my own experiences together much earlier than I did. It took me far too long to realize that I did not need to operate one day as a consultant concerned with management effectiveness and another as a consultant concerned with effective learning. I was similarly more tardy than I need have been in challenging in print fundamental issues about the definition of management development. I happily adhered for too many years to a definition of management development that was fundamentally the same as that produced by the Training Agency in 1977:

An attempt to improve managerial effectiveness through a planned and deliberate learning process.

Yet much of my own work showed that a great deal of management development was *not* planned and deliberate. The fact that managers learned in an informal and accidental way did not mean that we should not include this in our understanding of management development. The problem was that management development specialists and personnel directors were defining management development as to do with those things that they could influence through systems, policies and procedures.

I now leave out 'planned and deliberate' from the definition of management development. (See my book *Management Development: Strategies for Action* (IPM, 2nd Edition, 1993) for more on this.)

It was not until my research with directors that I was forced to face the reality of my own experience and for the first time both to challenge the definition and to offer, as I had never done before, a model! In fact, I had set out on the research project with the deliberate intention not only of describing the reality of the ways in which directors had been developed, but of producing a model. I did so because I recognized that I had never done this and thought it would be a good discipline for myself to do so. The result, first published in 1987, was the three-type model (Fig. 8.2).

What I did not see, but now assert, is that a learning organization:

• Will recognize and use all three types
• Will be especially concerned to convert type 1 into type 2

Converting Task into Learning

The process of thinking is facilitated in the design and implementation of my programmes in three stages:

1. Revans developed an equation to express the nature of learning as:

$$L = P + Q$$
$$\text{(Learning)} \quad \text{(Programmed knowledge)} \quad \text{(Questioning and problem-centred analysis)}$$

I expected (but did not receive) the wrath of Jehovah to fall on me when I sent Reg Revans a copy of the article in which I proposed that this equation should be changed to:

$$Q + P + Q = L.$$

The phenomenon I am describing is that it is asking questions and looking at problems that creates the demand for programmed knowledge, which in turn stimulates further questioning and probing; and it is the combination of those three stages that leads to learning.

Type 1: 'Informal managerial'—accidental processes

Characteristics   —occur within managerial activities
                      —explicit intention is task performance
                      —no clear development objectives
                      —unstructured in development terms
                      —not planned in advance
                      —owned by managers
Development   —learning is real, direct, unconscious,
consequences   insufficient

Type 2: 'Integrated managerial'—opportunistic processes

Characteristics   —occur within managerial activities
                      —explicit intention both task performance
                        and development
                      —clear development objectives
                      —structured for development by boss and
                        subordinate
                      —planned beforehand or reviewed
                        subsequently as learning experiences
                      —owned by managers
Development   —learning is real, direct, conscious,
consequences   more substantial

**Type 3: 'Formal management development'—planned
processes**

Characteristics   —often away from normal managerial
                        activities
                      —explicit intention is development
                      —clear development objectives
                      —structured for development by
                        developers
                      —planned beforehand or reviewed
                        subsequently as learning experiences
                      —owned more by developers than
                        managers
Development   —learning may be real (through a job) or
consequences   detached (through a course)
                      —is more likely to be conscious, relatively
                        infrequent

Figure 8.2   Types of management development
Source: A. Mumford, *Developing Top Managers*, Gower, 1988

2. A derivation of that approach is the idea that all managerial activities are potentially learning opportunities. It is not just the huge, unique, dramatic events that create learning—it can sometimes be relatively small things or combinations of small things. Hence the idea that we need to focus on activities as opportunities—in effect, conversion from type 1 to type 2 managers in the model.

3. Another characteristic of my work is that there has to be an explicit learning process as a general model (the learning cycle), and explicit individual understanding by each person of her or his preferred way of learning (the missing third, in many examples of action learning).

9

How Directors Learn from Experience

The learning cycle and learning styles provide one way of describing how directors learn. This chapter reviews additional ideas developed through my research.

In 1986 I carried out the first research in the United Kingdom on how directors had been developed for that role. (Nor had there been any research in the United States.) The project proceeded through interviews with 144 directors in 41 different organizations in Britain. With one exception, all the participants were on the main board.

Don Stradling, Graham Robinson and I formed the project team, and we interviewed directors at their business locations. In our report (*Developing Directors: The Learning Processes*), published in January 1987, we found among other things that:

- Most directors had learned through a mixture of relatively accidental and unstructured experiences. Systems of management development had not been widely influential.
- Management development systems had sometimes failed in whole or in part. This had occurred where they were insufficiently attached to the real concerns of managers and directors, were not strongly related to other planning processes in the business, and offered too little in terms of perceived return to managers participating in them.
- Neither the organizations nor the individual directors had fully recognized the opportunities for development while actually managing. Management development had too often been seen as a process separate from management practice.
- In some cases systems of development had not met their full potential because of a failure to set clear objectives for the management development process. This had created a consequential inability to assess results derived from the formal management development system.
- The learning process in general, and the individual's

reaction to learning, had been insufficiently understood, especially by the providers of formal processes for learning.

We proposed the Three Types, a new model of management development mentioned in the previous chapter (Fig. 8.2).

This was by far the biggest and most ambitious research project with which I had been involved. People at the time were astonished at my temerity in suggesting it. However, the report did not generate the excitement, interest and action about which I fantasized as we wrote it.

Its publication coincided with that of two other major reports, one produced by Charles Handy (*The Making of Managers*, NEDO, 1987), dealing with international comparisons on the development of managers, and one by John Constable, whose report was titled, *The Making of British Managers* (British Institute of Management, 1987). Projected and promoted with tremendous enthusiasm by their clients— (the National Economic Development Office, the CBI and the Department of Employment), these reports created a splash, the ripples of which are still visible on the waters of management development today. I was most in sympathy with some aspects of Charles Handy's report—not least because what he and his colleagues found in Japan was very similar to what we described as type 2 management development.

These two reports together led to the creation of the Management Charter Initiative and a major push for competency-based management education. The associated massive expansion of MBA programmes, based on comparative figures from the United States, caused me more chuckles than tears. How characteristic of a failure to learn effectively, that we should choose as our model the American MBA programmes, already the subject of much criticism there, while at the time the triumphant economies were those of Japan and Germany, two countries that did not provide MBA programmes at all!

Perhaps I should not have been surprised that conventional management development thinking should seize eagerly on targets connected with courses, rather than on the much less easily identified proposal in my report for using on-the-job opportunities more effectively. You could, after all, measure how many more MBA students the system was pumping out—whereas how would you measure whether managers were learning more effectively on the job?

Developing Directors did not sink entirely without trace, since it led to case 4, and by extension to my other director development programmes. There is yet another paradox in that the main enquiries that arose from the report were for off-the-job courses of development, rather than for work on how to improve development on the job.

While this report had no major national impact, it made a lot of difference to my own work. It raised my eyes above the particular experiences I had had, and the views I had developed, about the relevance of formal management training, and of the impact of both management training and broader management development schemes. The research showed that my own experiences, which had gradually caused me to become much less optimistic about the benefits of formal training and development, were sustained on a much wider scale in the research. Although there were examples of directors whose development had been significantly aided by formal management training or education, there were at least as many more for whom similar experiences had not led to development. We could not find a single case among the 41 organizations where the management development specialist or personnel director had actually evaluated the success of schemes in general, as distinct from evaluating particular courses. The project gave me the opportunity, or perhaps even forced me, to provide statements about the causes of effectiveness in management development and the model of types of management development, which I would never have done otherwise.

I had been encouraged by my client (the Manpower Services Commission) and by the principal of my business school, Gordon Wills, to write a book based on the research, but extending into a wider analysis of how directors could be developed. I wanted to call the book *Making it to the Top*, but the Marketing Department of my publisher ruled this out on the grounds that it sounded too much like an airport book. *Developing Top Managers* is still the only substantial wide-ranging and research-based book on the subject. It was given good reviews, has proved to be a nice reference point in sales situations for me—and has even been referred to in other books on management development.

Finally, the project and report produced something that had not been anticipated, because, unlike many research reports, it did not conclude by saying that further research should be conducted. My client at the Manpower Services Commission, once the initial flurry of excitement over Handy and Constable had passed, asked what could be done to provide further illustrations to directors of how they could learn from experience, since this had been such a major part of the original report.

Making Experience Count

Peter Honey joined Graham Robinson and myself on the resulting project, which was eventually published as *Directors' Development Guidebook: Making Experience Count* (Director Publications) in 1990. We found 21 directors in 15 organizations willing to participate in discussion and analysis with us about their real-work experiences, and how they were learning from them.

Whereas our first research had been based on single interviews with directors and organizational representatives, our new research involved meetings with individuals three or four times over a three-month period. We first got them to talk about the work activities in which they had been involved in the period since we had last met them. Then we helped them focus on what they had learned and how they had learned it. The terms of reference for the project were that we should produce a practical working document, not a research report. The aim was not merely to analyse what the directors had learned, or even how they had learned it, but to develop ideas on how directors could learn more effectively from their normal work experiences.

We started with one hypothesis: that, while most people learned mainly by looking at experiences *retrospectively*, learning could be enhanced if people recognized in advance the kind of learning that could occur through their work and planned better to learn from those opportunities as and when they arose. We hoped to find good illustrations of how learning could better be achieved through thinking ahead—*prospectively*. The advantage of having participants start from their experiences, rather than getting them to describe the learning they had achieved, was demonstrated when we found that the hypothesis was an insufficient and indeed misleading statement about how the learning actually occurred. We found not two but four ways in which directors learned from work experience, as shown in Fig. 9.1.

- Intuitive
- Incidental
- Retrospective
- Prospective

Figure 9.1   The four approaches to managerial learning from experience
Source: A. Mumford, P. Honey and G. Robinson, *Directors' Development Guidebook*, Director Publications, 1990

The Four Approaches to Managerial Learning

The fully detailed explanation of these four approaches is set out in the *Directors' Development Guidebook*. The following summary gives a basic introduction to each of the approaches:

The Intuitive Approach

The Intuitive approach involves learning from experience, but not through a conscious process. The person using intuitive learning claims that learning is an inevitable consequence of having experiences. If questioned, he or she is able to talk in detail about a variety of different experiences describing what happened and what was achieved. However, people using this approach find it difficult, and unnecessary, to articulate what they learned or how they learned it. They are content that learning occurs 'naturally'.

> 'I suspect you are doing it all the time without realizing you're doing so.'

Since people using the Intuitive approach put their trust in learning as a 'natural', effortless process, they find it difficult to accept that there are advantages to be gained by making the process more deliberate and conscious, either for themselves or for other people.

The Incidental Approach

The Incidental approach involves learning by chance from activities that jolt an individual into conducting a 'post mortem'. A variety of things can act as jolts, but common ones are when something out of the ordinary crops up or where something has not gone according to plan. Mishaps and frustrations often provide the spur.

When something hits people using Incidental learning between the eyes, they are inclined to mull over what happened in an informal, unstructured way. They tend to use the benefit of hindsight as a way of rationalizing, even justifying, what has happened.

> 'I learn from the unfamiliar parts of my job, not from the bits I am already familiar with and have already mastered.'

One difference from the Intuitive approach is that people using incidental learning find it easier to conduct post mortems by talking things over with someone else.

The Retrospective Approach

The Retrospective approach involves learning from experience by looking back over what happened and reaching conclusions about it in a more structured way. The Retrospective approach reviews mishaps and mistakes, but in addition, lessons are drawn from routine events and successes. Learning is extracted from a diverse range of small and large, positive and negative experiences.

People using the Retrospective approach conduct reviews, sometimes in their heads, sometimes in conversation and sometimes on paper. The sequence looks like this:

| Something has happened | It is reviewed | Conclusions are reached |

The outcome in the Retrospective approach is that considered conclusions are knowingly reached. An individual, by reviewing, acquires knowledge, skills and insights or has them confirmed and reinforced.

'Reviewing is essential to put things in perspective.'

The Prospective Approach

The Prospective approach involves all the Retrospective elements, but includes an additional dimension. Whereas Retrospection concentrates on reviewing what happened *after* an experience, the Prospective approach includes planning to learn *before* an experience. Future events are seen not merely as things to be done, which are important in their own right, but also as opportunities to learn.

The sequence in Prospective learning is:

| Plan to learn | Implement the plan | Review the plan | Reach conclusions |

'There is no substitute for thorough planning, not only to get things done but also to learn from doing them.'

The interviews produced fascinating experiences themselves illustrative of the four approaches. One director went courteously through the process of settling me down, talking about the weather and getting me a cup of tea before saying 'Now just remind me, what are we going to talk about?' When I reminded him that we were going to discuss what he had been doing over the last three or four weeks he looked first startled and then thoughtful. 'The most important things, you say. Well now ... Perhaps I had better look in my diary; there really isn't anything that springs to mind.' If I had asked him what he had learned, presumably he would have been even more bewildered! At the other extreme, we found directors who picked up our suggestion about keeping a learning log. One or two even had typed notes which they used in discussion with us.

The *Guidebook* was supported by a variety of experiences from different individuals and from different situations. Subsequently we found a particularly interesting example of how individuals learned differently from the same experience, and this is a particularly powerful way of illustrating the four approaches.

The Management Meeting Case

A regular management meeting was held with a long but fairly familiar routine agenda. The last item, however, was a serious non-routine problem raised by a director, concerning overruns on a major project and associated activities. However, there was not enough time left to discuss the problem properly.

Four of the directors were asked afterwards:

1. What had happened in relation to that item
2.. What they thought about what had happened
3. Whether they learned anything from what had happened

The responses of the four were as follows.

Personnel Director
'I found it a very frustrating meeting. I raised the problem beforehand with the chief executive, and asked for good time to discuss it. But there was nothing resolved because we didn't have time. We will have to meet again, perhaps setting up a special meeting. Next time, I will suggest that we discuss this issue much earlier in the meeting, even before the routine items.' (Incidental)

Chief Executive
'I was trying deliberately to generate a different style of discussion. I wanted a much more open-ended process than we usually have, and most importantly, I was aiming to get consensus rather than just people forcing me to make a decision. I wanted to see whether we could work that way, and what I would need to do to make it work. Though I thought beforehand I would learn something from this experiment, I certainly did!' (Prospective)

Manufacturing Director
'All the meetings are like that. It's nothing new really that we have that sort of problem and then we cannot discuss it and get a decision. There must be a better way! I suppose I picked up some facts about the problem, if that is what you call learning.' (Intuitive)

Marketing Director
'It was all part of our general problem over meetings. [He quoted a number of similar cases.] We don't sort out our priorities. I have been looking back at some of our other meetings, both with the chief executive and with my own people, and I think we have the same sort of problem. Not all of them have the kind of excitement that was generated on this one, because it was so urgent, but basically it is the same issue. What are the priorities for our attention?' (Retrospective)

One of the interesting questions that arose in our research was the extent to which any individual director was dominated by one approach. We did find individuals who were prone to use only one of the four approaches, whatever the situation. This was especially true of two directors who were substantially dominated by the Intuitive approach. This suggests that some directors are as limited in their approach to learning from experience as others are by their preferred learning style. Just as with learning styles, however, we take the view that it is possible to build additional strengths—to shift at least part of the way along the continuum—so that someone using the Intuitive approach does at least occasionally pick up the Incidental approach, and the Retrospective approach can sometimes be shifted towards the Prospective approach.

This is an area in which the comment made above that 'More research is needed' is certainly relevant. I found confirming examples in later research on learning from difficulty. Larger numbers would provide greater assurance about the findings, or perhaps lead to an adjustment. Are there really only four approaches? It would also be useful to establish whether there are correlations between learning style preferences and likelihood of using one of the four approaches.

As shown at the end of this chapter, however, the four approaches' construct does say something important about the learning organization.

Developing Knowledge, Skills and Insights

Historically, the focus in formal management development has been primarily on what managers and directors need to learn, rather than how they learned it. The first UK business schools followed US practice in focusing on content—what managers need to know—rather than on how they learn it. The same can be said of competence-based programmes for management development, especially but not uniquely pushed by the Management Charter Initiative—again, a system, discipline or philosophy invented in the United States, most memorably by Richard Boyatzis.

In our second project, we were concerned not with what directors should learn, but with what they actually had learned from the experiences they described to us. When we analysed the experiences, we decided against using any of the alternative constructs for competences. There was no existing statement which we thought appropriate for directors, and in any event the director population for whom we were writing the *Guidebook* would be more likely to understand and use terms like 'knowledge', 'skills' and 'attitudes.' Our analysis of experience was able to distinguish the first two quite satisfactorily, but we found that the word 'attitudes' was not evocative of what our interviewees were telling us. So we replaced 'attitude' with 'insight'. Of course, the categories are not exclusive—any experience can involve all three.

Knowledge

This is the acquisition of data or information. Sometimes it is not new knowledge but confirmation of past information. For example:

> 'Visiting Korea and Japan expanded my experience of different countries and companies, and is helping me to deal with other nationalities outside the UK.'
> 'I had never attended a board meeting before, and I had no idea about how things were conducted. Who did what? What should I say, and when should I say it? I learned a lot about aspects of the business I had never been involved with, e.g. legal aspects.'

Skills

These are the means directors use to carry out their work effectively. The most obvious examples include making decisions, running meetings, negotiating. For example:

> 'I have tended to treat professional people as rather different from the ones I normally deal with in management. When I saw how X managed the relationship, however, I saw that he was much more business-like in setting up a timetable and targets for performance. I learned from seeing him do it, and it has certainly paid off for me since in similar situations.'

'I constantly find that I am so busy that I do not have time to review what I have done. I know this is a mistake, so I am firmly setting aside 30 minutes every Friday—and I got my secretary to help me stick to my new resolve.'

Insights

This is about perceptiveness; some people would call it developing wisdom. You can acquire knowledge and skills but lack the extra dimension provided through insight. Insights are often expressed as conclusions; they help you generalize from particular experiences. For example:

'I am a creative thinker, and I like listening to other people's ideas, but also throwing in my own. The problem as chief executive is that quite often people do not see them as ideas that I am genuinely interested to have discussed, but see them as proposals. They either get all defensive about them, or rush away and do them.'

'In my previous company we had used brain-storming quite a bit. In my new company we used a different version of it recently on the question of financial rewards. The important point was that I adapted my past experience and didn't simply repeat exactly the same process—and a lot of situations require that conversion.'

In all sorts of ways, learning is a question of interrelationships—between task and learning, between people. In this project we analysed the relationships that existed between the four approaches and the three types of learning. We found that the three 'hindsight' approaches (Intuitive, Incidental and Retrospective) involved all three types of learning, but that the largest proportion of experiences could be described as insight.

When we looked at the rather smaller number of achieved learning experiences generated through the Prospective approach, we found a balance between insight and knowledge. However, the Prospective approach was often a fairly generalized view about an opportunity to learn something, rather than a specific statement of a knowledge, skill or insight that might be acquired. Logically, it would be rather difficult to say in advance what your insights are going to be! So, though you might be adopting a Prospective approach, i.e. thinking about learning in advance, the actual achievement of insight would be most often achieved in hindsight.

We constantly find that individuals are more prepared to give time to looking back rather than looking forward—three of the four approaches are obviously 'hindsight' approaches. Is it sensible to encourage the Prospective approach? A great deal of formal management development does talk about planning ahead in the sense of identifying courses or job moves. However, in this context, where we are talking about learning from work experience, is it either feasible or practical to try and urge people into more Prospective thinking? The case for doing so rests on two propositions.

The first is that there is a proportion of people who will, given sensible guidance, take up Prospective opportunities more frequently. Managers and directors do in fact spend a lot of time planning; the need is to associate the idea of planning for learning with other forms of planning that are undertaken, rather than to leave it as a unique discipline associated only with learning.

The second proposition is that effective use of learning from work experiences really requires improved systems and personal discipline. While for many people it is entirely sensible to start from the three 'hindsight' approaches, it is then desirable to encourage people to think ahead. What actually seems to happen, as suggested earlier, is that they improve the quantity and quality of their hindsight learning. I have to say that it is much easier to get directors on to the hindsight tasks than it is to get them on to the Prospective approach. It is a struggle; it has to be conducted very much on a person-to-person basis or in pairs if you are on a course. It has to be specific—what are you doing over the next weeks which might provide a learning opportunity? Simply setting people the task of doing this does not work; they need guidance through checklists, exercises and personal workbooks (see Chapter 17).

We generated some data that have particular resonance for the learning organization. One of the crucial questions about learning is the nature and viability of generalization from any particular learning experience. It is one of the virtues of the learning cycle that it draws out the steps necessary in order to secure effective generalization—but also emphasizes that rushing from a collection of data to planning action without a 'concluding' stage is likely to be ineffective. Analysis of our data enables us to reach some conclusions about generalization! The good news is that 75 per cent of the 'hindsight' experiences have application beyond the particular situation described, contrasted with the 25 per cent which were learning experiences relevant only to a narrow and specific circumstance which was unlikely to be repeated. This is not to say that all the generalizations might be accurate and viable—it is unfortunately possible for people to reach the wrong conclusion!

While the good news from this analysis is that generalization does follow in so many cases, this does not provide an answer to a different question. If the generalization were accurate and viable, it could enhance the individual's capacity to apply learning within the organization. One possibility, however, would be that the generalization would apply only within that organization and would not be generalizable elsewhere. This raises an interesting question about the learning organization. Is the learning that is developed, encouraged and sustained for the purposes of the organization transferable to another organization? Should it be? Or is the real point that what should be transferable is not the *content* of learning but the *process* of learning achieved in any organization?

Triggers for Learning

I frequently use with directors an exercise in which I ask them first to identify the most significant, important or helpful learning experiences they have had, and then to identify the least helpful experiences. While this has great practical virtue in terms of both the time available and my overall objectives with the individual, the analysis of data from this research has shown that analysis with a different purpose produces understandably a different result.

A research process enabled us to look at all the experiences reported, and all the learning that individuals derived from those experiences. We were not therefore involved so much in highlighting, one consequence of which is that people tend inevitably to pick out the most unusual, and by definition the most important, experiences they have had. Because we were able to analyse the total range of responses, we were interested to find that, for example, there was a 50–50 split between whether the experience was in a wholly new activity or in one that was familiar. In many ways this is good news, because it emphasizes how much people do not have to be focused on novel or exciting changes of task, job or circumstance. Indeed, it indicates how much more there is still to learn from relatively familiar circumstances—thus supporting the argument advanced earlier in this book about the desirability of building from incremental rather than from transformational theories about learning.

Another version of this argument was derived from testing the experiences to see if they were as we described them relatively routine or blockbuster in nature: 70 per cent of the hindsight experiences really fitted the routine categorization, and 90 per cent of the experiences from the Prospective approach were in this category, no doubt because people do not envisage blockbuster learning experiences in advance.

It should be remembered again that all this analysis is derived from work experiences—it is of course quite possible that an analysis of experience on courses would produce a different set of approaches.

Learning from Difficulty—a Major Trigger

Learning for most directors, most of the time, is based on task requirements and situational opportunities. Sometimes they learn because they recognize what they need to learn, and a small proportion learn by planning to do so in advance. More frequently, they learn from tasks and situations that have occurred which they did not envisage as learning opportunities. Predominant among these are the experiences which they variously describe as 'learning from something that didn't work', 'learning from a failure'. Much less frequently, they identify a success as a major learning experience. On the whole, however, they do not look at successes because they do not need to; if something has worked, given the normal pressures on your time, there is no priority in delving into why it has worked and therefore into what you have learned from the success.

This can lead to problems, because failing to go round the task and learning cycles in relation to a success often means that the learning is partial, and may be inappropriately applied in a different situation. Although it is desirable to encourage managers and directors to look at successes and really work out what they have learned from them, and I do this, the reality is that most of them learn more frequently from difficulties, disasters and failures. Given this psychological disposition, it is sensible at least to advise them on how to do this more effectively.

I was asked by Bryan Smith at Sundridge Park Management Centre to participate with him on a study in this area. Brian's original idea was to call it 'Learning from Failure', but when he involved me in the project we agreed to call it 'Learning from Difficulty', because we felt the word 'failure' was too harsh and too restricting. The main part of the research was a series of interviews conducted with 50 managers and directors. A particularly interesting subgroup comprised a number of directors who had been made redundant. I am grateful to Brian and to Sundridge Park for allowing me to use the material produced by the research, which attempted to answer, in relation to learning from difficulty:

Familiar	Same function or basic role in same organization
Part familiar	Same function or role in a different organization Different function or role in same organization
Unfamiliar	New function or role in a different organization

Figure 9.2   Types of job change
Source: A. Mumford, *Management Development: Strategies for Action*, 2nd ed, IPM, 1993

- When did they learn?
- Why did they learn?
- What did they learn?
- How did they learn?

When Did They Learn?

By far the largest number of examples occurred at times of significant job change.

Personal relationships, which we expected might have generated 'difficulty', scarcely ever arose in managers' comments. The major exception was in relationship to bosses, where personal relationships did cause difficulties. Changes in organizational culture and in adapting different national cultures also caused problems.

The changes of job in which the interviewees were involved came from a promotion or a sideways move to a job at a similar level. Figure 9.2 illustrates the types of job change. The following are representative examples of difficulty experienced:

'I have moved from an organization which often encouraged people to say "I can't" to one in which you were expected to say "I can". It was a problem to recognize and cope with this.'

'I felt very vulnerable in one major aspect of my new job. It was in a side of the business in which I had never worked before.'

'It was my first at board level. I was the only woman on the board. My contribution was devalued by a number of aggressive men.'

'My new boss wanted me to change the priorities and focus of my job dramatically.'

'My boss was an F&F man—he managed by Fear and Favourites.'

'I encountered a difficulty in Asia which I had not fully appreciated before. They are so eager to please that they will promise things they have no ability to achieve.'

Why Did They Learn?

Most of the participants said they had worked for organizations that were more likely to be unhelpful than helpful in exposing and learning from difficulties. Examples included:

'You are not expected to ask for help.'
'Difficulty was seen as weakness.'
'It was thought to be disloyal if you discussed problems outside your immediate unit.'

Some organizations provided a more positive environment:

'Trying and failing was not a capital offence in that organization—perhaps because it was American.'

Bosses were sometimes more helpful than the organization in general:

'He had a relaxed attitude to people taking initiative and risks so long as there were no surprises when things went wrong.'

Most desirable of all:

'When I made a mistake my boss said, "What have we learned from it?"'

But of course, there were bosses who did not help:

'You could not discuss difficulties with my boss because he simply refused to hear bad news.'
'He was so heavy on mistakes that he created fear and concealment.'

What Did They Learn?

We logged 178 statements about skills, knowledge or insight that individuals had obtained from difficult situations. There was very little overlap—there is no single neat list to be presented. The most interesting statements for this project concerned:

• What they learned about themselves
• What they learned about other people

Respondents felt that such knowledge would help them to manage difficult situations in the future. For example:

'I know more about when to ask for advice.'
'When you are working in a different country, assume everyone will be different, not the same.'

'I learned that a boss could be frightened of his subordinates.'
'One of the things I learned from these cases was when to be assertive and when not.'

How Did They Learn?

As was the case on the two previous research projects described above, the interview situation brought out for many managers the fact that they had not learned as well as they might have done close to the event. Few of them had encountered managers of the type quoted above who said, 'So what have we learned from this?' Although 60 per cent of our participants said they had tried to think through what they had learned on their own, our view was that this figure almost certainly overstated the reality. Few managers have been given the concepts and tools necessary for them to improve their capacity to understand what is involved in their own methods of learning. Only two of the 50 interviewees actually mentioned the discipline they used to review and record their own learning:

> 'I keep a weekly written review of what I have been doing and what I have learned from it. It is more a Management Review than a learning log.'
> 'I have a file marked "Learning". I just throw in notes I have made, ideas that have occurred to me. Every few months I pull out the file and look over what is in it.'

About a third said they had shared and learned with colleagues; only a quarter said they had learned with and from a boss. In addition, the emphasis in such discussions was mainly on the problem and the difficulty, rather than on what was being learned from it. Learning tended to be an implicit consequence rather than an explicit purpose of these discussions—not a surprising phenomenon, but important in terms of the quality and depth of learning actually achieved.

Emotional Issues

Nearly a third of the participants said they had experienced a relatively extreme form of emotion, such as fear and pain, during difficult situations; rather more agreed they had felt anxiety. However, this was seen by them neither as a major motivating force for learning, nor a significant drag on it.

Learning from Other People's Difficulties

Of special significance to organization learning is the question of whether managers are able to identify things they have learned from difficulties experienced by their colleagues. Only 30 per cent in this study had done so—which can be attributed to the fact that the idea of learning by observation has as yet rarely been properly encouraged and developed in managers.

Relation to the Four Approaches

As part of this project, participants were given an exercise on the four approaches, asking them to identify which approach they were most likely to adopt in learning from experience. Responses showed they were most likely to use the Retrospective approach and least likely to use the Prospective approach. Since the nature of difficulties can often be predicted, the potential for using the Prospective approach more in the learning-from-difficulty context is clear. It might often, of course, match the kind of 'blockbuster' definition referred to earlier in this chapter.

Some Conclusions from the Project

Since learning from difficulty has a clear association with a manager's imperative to perform more effectively—and is also a frequently encountered experience—there are strong reasons for striving to improve the capacity of individuals, and through them of groups and organizations, to learn more appropriately from problems, difficulties, failures—even, at the extreme, disasters. Improved learning results if individuals, groups and organizations:

- Establish a better organizational climate for learning, and establish a more helpful relationship between bosses and subordinates in order to facilitate learning
- Encourage the use of colleagues as aids to learning
- Provide individuals with an understanding of the disciplined sequence for learning, and of their own preferred methods of learning

10

Diagnosing the Learning Organization

My experience of trying to interpret and facilitate actions appropriate to a learning organization started before the cases referred to so far.

CASE 9

In this company I was responsible for management development. I provided directly management training courses for middle and senior managers, and recommended the use of external management education courses such as Henley and Harvard. I was also responsible for designing and redesigning the system and form for the individual performance and development review. Copies of all the forms were returned to me, and I kept score of how many completed forms had been returned and by which departments, divisions and regions by 1 July, the date set at the beginning of the annual process.

As an associated activity, I ran the Management Training Department. In my later years of responsibility, we actually had to have a rationing arrangement because most of the courses I ran were so popular—so we distributed nominations around the various units; if a unit did not take up its allocation, judicious comments were made both informally and if necessary formally to fill the gaps in their nominations.

All of this was within a context that explicitly valued training. The organization was well known for what it did in management training and development; indeed, I was pursued by head hunters at a time when this flattering process was in its infancy in the United Kingdom. Measured by the beliefs of directors about the virtue of training and of the annual identification of development needs, we were certainly good at management development as it was then understood.

The beliefs espoused by the directors were given most prominent form when the company secured its biggest ever contract. The project director had previously been nominated to attend a new internal course, the most senior to be run at that time. It was naturally assumed that the priority demands of this huge project would mean that he would be taken off the course. However, the managing director insisted that he stay on it. He did not want to set the precedent of people being withdrawn—and the absence of this precedent was one that we employed with great success whenever afterwards someone else claimed to be too busy to attend a major course.

This substantial history of management training provided an excellent base when the Industrial Training Boards were set up. We were able to maximize our grants, and indeed more than pay for the cost of training, because we were able to meet the training board requirements—the existence of systems, the number of people being trained, the fact that job descriptions had been written for all our managers. Our training board at the time reminded me of a description I had read by an American historian of George III, of whom it was said: 'He did his best according to his lights, which were however few and dim'—but we liked getting the grants!

Although good in its time, this was not, however, a learning organization.

Obligatory Training Days

The United Kingdom has imported a number of management development practices and ideas from the United States. By the mid-1980s, the then Manpower Services Commission, as it began to emphasize the importance of management development, became enthusiastic about the idea of obligatory training days. Some American companies, and IBM in Britain of course, were a visible example to us; IBM decided that all its managers should attend management training for a given number of days per year.

Potentially, this provided another way of measuring whether a company was 'doing enough' in management development. Was it setting a target? Were its managers meeting it? I vigorously opposed the idea of a required number of off-the-job training days. The Manpower Services Commission itself changed its early definition from 'training' to 'learning', and began to talk about different ways of meeting a target. Eventually the idea of a quantified target of this kind, originally considered for the Management Charter Initiative (MCI) Code of Practice, was abandoned. That Code of Practice could, however, have been seen as a contributor to views about the learning organization. The ten points in the Code constituted a statement about what an organization that wanted to provide good management development should be doing—and therefore clearly also gave a means of evaluating the extent to which the organization was actually meeting the requirements of the Code.

It would be interesting to know whether those organizations now claiming that they are on the way to becoming learning organizations have at least subscribed to the MCI Code—and whether they have made any connection between the Code and their understanding of the learning organization.

In any event, the Code of Practice deals with only some of the requirements for a learning organization.

Understanding What You Are Looking For

Assessment of the learning organization has to be focused on learning. It is not about a collection of desirable *general management* values and practices: it is about practices that identifiably and directly facilitate *learning*. It is also, of course, about learning in all its splendidly variable forms—not just about the formal delivery of courses or other structured forms of development.

Case Experience in Diagnosing the Learning Organization

In Chapters 1 and 2 I have shown how my diagnostic approach provides evidence about:

• Individual development needs
• Group development needs
• Other issues of management significance

In only one organization (case 7) have I explicitly referred to the learning organization—and in that example the reference was to answers on the Learning Diagnostic Questionnaire (see below), and to how some proposed actions would facilitate a learning organization or sub-organization.

In the other cases, data relevant to learning organization behaviours and practices have been collected, but not as an explicit diagnostic tool for the learning organization.

In the examples of the creation of personal development plans, the interviews produced information about the experiences these individuals have gone through, particularly within their existing organizations. Respondents described formal and informal development experiences, and this gives evidence on how supportive the organization or their part of it has been of learning and development.

Further information comes my way from listening to the participants on my director development programmes. There are two different sources. Since the programmes are designed around real themes and problems of current relevance to the participants, I hear the way in which they refer to their existing processes for tackling and particularly discussing problems in the real world. This tells me something about their approach to learning, and especially the constraints and inhibitions they suffer in attempting to learn, in their real-work context. They do not talk about it directly in terms of learning but rather in terms of not being able to raise issues, not being able to be open, a lack of trust, a punitive attitude to mistakes. Since learning is also an explicit issue on all these programmes, we discuss, often through the Learning Diagnostic Questionnaire, results on how far the work environment is supportive of learning. Finally, of course, there are those comments made to me over coffee, drinks and meals which add to my understanding of what their work context is really like.

Examples of comments made in these different situations include:

'Of course, if we had really taken time to reflect properly on what went wrong last time, we would not be repeating the mistake now.'

'We all appraise our people every year, but [the Chief Executive] does not appraise us.'

'We simply do not share information and views enough. We only meet at Executive meetings. We ought to meet more often, though informally.'

'Your programme is the only occasion when we get together and talk about big issues seriously.'

Specific Measures of the Learning Organization

For convenience, my definition of the learning organization is repeated here:

The learning organization is one that creates an environment where the behaviours and practices involved in continuous development are actively encouraged.

I have two methods through which I, or a client, can assess the extent to which the organization meets that definition. I use Fig. 10.1 when I have a short period of time on a course, and have not been able to give people the Learning Diagnostic Questionnaire (LDQ) in advance, or on one occasion when the full Learning Diagnostic Questionnaire was thought to be too formidable by the client. I say something like:

'I just want to raise the general issue about organizational learning; your full LDQ raises more issues than we can cope with. I just want to make you aware that there is something called a learning organization.'

An organization can be said to encourage learning when:

- It encourages managers to identify their own learning needs
- It provides a regular review of performance and learning for the individual
- It encourages managers to assess challenging learning goals for themselves
- It provides feedback at the time, both on performance and on achieved learning
- It reviews the performance of managers in helping to develop others
- It assists managers to see learning opportunities on the job
- It seeks to provide new experiences from which managers can learn
- It provides or facilitates the use of training on the job
- It tolerates some mistakes provided managers try to learn from them
- It encourages managers to review, conclude and plan learning activities
- It encourages managers to change their traditional ways of doing things

Figure 10.1   A learning culture
Source: P. Honey and A. Mumford, *Manual of Learning Opportunities*, Honey, 1989

From Fig. 10.1 managers can be asked to assess their own unit or the complete organization on a scale of 0 to 10 on how well it meets these statements.

The Learning Diagnostic Questionnaire

Through the cases reviewed in this book and others not contained here, I have gradually become more aware of the total learning context in which individuals are trying to develop themselves. I worked with Peter Honey on a questionnaire which focused specifically on this aspect. As with the Learning Styles Questionnaire, the Learning Diagnostic Questionnaire offers questions about managerial behaviour. Some are directly about learning; others are less direct but identifiably relevant.

At Peter's suggestion, we added two additional dimensions to my original idea of testing the individual's work environment. We decided also to look at the skills of learning possessed by individuals, and at the attitudes and emotions they had which might encourage or constrain their responsiveness to learning opportunities. We thought that for most purposes it would be more acceptable and convenient if we had one questionnaire that covered all three elements, rather than having three further questionnaires to add to the Learning Styles Questionnaire.

The Learning Diagnostic Questionnaire offers 20 paired items relevant to the learning organization, requiring respondents to tick the statement that most closely applies. Examples are:

In my organization there is a systematic process for identifying development needs.	In my organization the identification of development needs is rather haphazard.
I work in an organization where it's OK to say you don't know, and/or to be open about your problems.	I work in an organization where it's not OK to admit you don't know and/or that you have problems.
My organization tends to encourage people to conform and stick to the rules.	My organization tends to encourage people to experiment and try different ways of doing things.

There are norms created from the response of, so far, 557 British managers to the questionnaire.

Compared with the other inputs mentioned above providing a view about the organization as an effective home for learning, the LDQ ensures that all participants are responding to the same questions. Because I work largely with small groups of senior managers and directors, the organizational picture is partial rather than complete—it is a picture of that particular group, not of the total organization. It does provide a valuable insight for that group; but, even more valuably, it indicates differences between individuals. This is illustrated below for a group of 10 senior managers.

[Responses to Learning Diagnostic Questionnaire]

Rating of working situation	Number of responses
Very high	1
High	2
Moderate	5
Low	1
Very low	1

The point of analysis here was first the extraordinary difference between the extreme views of Very Low and Very High, and second the number of Moderate ratings. I described the results to the director of this group (himself with a Moderate score) as providing a good deal of scope for improvement in the working situation, in terms of how it facilitated learning.

As with learning styles, the view of Honey and myself has been that any diagnostic instrument that simply leaves people with a diagnosis is not good enough.

Like the Learning Styles Questionnaire, the Learning Diagnostic Questionnaire indicates changes in behaviour that would lead to an improved rating of the organization as a learning context. Ways of achieving this are spelled out in a personal workbook, *The Opportunist Learner*. In this, each question is described and possible responses leading to improvement are indicated. As an example, we deal with one of the questions illustrated above as follows:

I work in an organization where it's OK to say you don't know and/or to be open about your problems.	I work in an organization where it's not OK to admit you don't know and/or that you have problems.

In the workbook we say:

> Working in a culture where it is OK to say you don't know and/or to be open about problems makes learning respectable. Organizations where everyone is expected to know all the answers and to get things right 100% of the time puts the impossible strain of being infallible on everyone. This unrealistic expectation forces people to pretend to be all-knowing and infallible and as a consequence not to be in learning mode.

Our suggestion is:

> Test it out by selecting a topic where being brave enough openly to declare your ignorance about something, and/or to admit to having a problem, will not seriously damage your credibility. Also, choose appropriate people to practise being open with.

Although so far I have used the LDQ only with relatively small groups, some organizations have taken it up as a diagnostic instrument covering a much larger range of managers—indeed, in one or two cases for their complete managerial population. It would be helpful to be able to report the results here, but unfortunately, as with the Learning Styles Questionnaire, dragging data out of enthusiasts is extraordinarily difficult.

11   Implications for the Learning Organization

Improving the Capacity to Learn

The research work and practical director development programmes reported here consistently tell the same story. Individuals do not have the skills, techniques and disciplines needed to learn most effectively. Managers talk about learning from experience, but in fact often acknowledge that they have learned less than they might have done.

Since individuals lack disciplined processes, it is not surprising that groups and even complete organizations do not learn effectively either. We have to get individual learning right before we can sensibly set grand and ambitious statements about organizational learning. But one-to-one relationships, groups and complete units can take aboard the same message and use the learning cycle, learning styles and the four approaches in developing their use of tasks as learning opportunities.

The Hierarchy in Operation

Figure 7.1 above introduced the learning hierarchy. In one organization in which I worked, the process of action learning was taken through three levels. One of the issues was how to respond to the question, 'Have we the competences to become world-class in manufacturing?'

Individual Level

Each manager and director established a personal development plan, referring to competences, issues, opportunities and problems.

One-to-One Relationships

The personal development plans were discussed with the individual's boss, and his or her agreement and help on the proposals contained within it was obtained. In addition, individuals worked in pairs on a workshop to refine and get further help from colleagues.

Groups

The group of managers involved decided to set up and manage for themselves a project that had two stages. The first stage entailed working out their answer to the question, 'What do we mean by world-class manufacturing; what are the criteria?' The second stage focused on designing a plan for managing the transition to meeting those criteria.

Organization Level

This involved a group of managers in one division of a company. The continued activities it embraced, for example, in carrying to middle- and lower-level managers the kind of process in which they had been involved was energized by the managers themselves. It would, however, be fair to say that this involved a sub-organization level, not the complete organization represented by the company as a whole.

Implications for the Learning Organization

The current literature on organizational learning insufficiently recognizes the levels of learning relationships in organizations. Even though Peter Senge has said that there is no organizational learning without effective individual learning, and has talked about the possibilities of team learning, his work and that of others has focused on the highest and most difficult level—the organization. In consequence, the literature has wholly underplayed the elements that have to be put in place before organizational learning can be achieved.

Conscious Learning— Individual and Organizational

Most individuals like 'finding out more about themselves'. The Learning Styles approach not only provides this, but leads to practical work on personal development. Similarly, the Learning Diagnostic Questionnaire, and the specifically learning organization questions within it, provides for the same kind of approach. 'Why are my answers like that? What can I do if I want to change them?'

One night at the National Theatre in London, Laurence Olivier gave one of his greatest performances as Othello. So extraordinary was he on this particular night that fellow-members of the cast and the supporting staff stood in the corridors back stage to applaud him back to his dressing room. He passed them without a word and closed the door to his dressing room. Eventually one of his colleagues went in to ask what was wrong. 'Larry this was marvellous—one of your very best performances. What is wrong now?' Olivier replied, 'I know it was great; the problem is I don't know how I did it.'

If managers were as effective in performance as Olivier was on that particular occasion, would we need to worry about whether they knew how they had done it? The answer must be that most cannot repeat their best work unless they know what made it best. My research and experience both show that directors and managers do in fact recognize that they need to be better at learning, and are quite prepared to take up more effective learning practices where they see these as relevant and valid—which means, built on the realities of their normal work. For this purpose, my research and diagnostic instruments, when brought together, will be particularly facilitative of improved organizational learning.

One of the major points of the research was that directors had not recognized during their careers that the experiences they had gone through were actually learning experiences. To say that all experiences are potentially learning experiences is valid for most managers most of the time. But they may not recognize the learning opportunity involved. Here is an example from the first director research project:

A large UK-based organization acquired a US-based business which itself had a multiplicity of subsidiaries. The main board director was sent out to visit the US companies after the acquisition, with the remit from his chief executive that broadly asked which subsidiaries should be kept, which should be sold as quickly as possible, and which should be put on 'hold'. The director involved mentioned this in his discussion with me as one of his major learning experiences—the different kinds of business involved, the fact that there were actually significant differences of management style although they were all run by Americans, the different procedures, systems and disciplines used. He could see why some companies were very profitable and others were not—but in other cases there was no clear reason.

As he discussed this experience with me he became quite excited and began to lean across the table and jab his finger at me. 'What you will be telling me is that this was a learning experience. And it obviously was. But I did not see that at the time. The chief executive and I just discussed the report and made our proposals to the main board. We never in any way discussed what I had learned—just what the recommendations were. He should have asked what I had learned. I should have told him. The personnel director should have come to see me and find out what I had learned. That's what you will be telling me.'

The fact is that a lot of learning opportunities are like that. They are not identified in advance (i.e. the Prospective approach is not adopted). Even worse, they are not recognized afterwards and squeezed for the learning they contain. Occasionally the general idea is grasped, so someone will be presented with a 'Big Opportunity'. Another example was a general manager who was sent off to Paris, having been told that it was a big change for him—different country, new company; 'you can add to your reputation'. No one talked about what he would do or learn.

A learning organization will not deal in generalizations. It will provide encouragement and support for specific behaviours and practices. It will want to manage learning opportunities in the way that it manages all other significant aspects of its work. It will certainly want to ensure that the specifics involved in a 'Big Opportunity' are spelled out. Big O is represented in Fig. 11.1; the process of defining and managing the smaller opportunities contained within it is illustrated in Fig. 11.2.

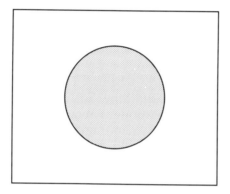

Figure 11.1   Big O
Source: A. Mumford, *How Managers Can Develop Managers*, Gower, 1993

Figure 11.2   Big O and smaller o's
Source: A. Mumford, *How Managers Can Develop Managers*, Gower, 1993

Figure 11.2 is even more meaningful in colour, because it brings out the fact that the specific smaller opportunities within Big O can differ in terms of size but also in terms of depth and intensity. With the general manager going to France, Big O should have been broken down into specific areas. The things he actually learned, which could have been specified, included:

- The way his French colleagues like to run meetings
- His French colleagues' approach to decision-making
- Their method of dealing with secretaries
- The nature of the market in France for his product
- The market elsewhere on the Continent
- Different processes for accessing these different markets

In discussion with me, the general manager was amazed at how much he had learned. Some of it he had recognized at the time and had been able to use then and subsequently. His comment on some other aspects was, 'I can identify now some things I learned, but I think I did not really recognize I had learned them at the time. So I probably hadn't learned them because I had not thought about them then.'

However, even encouraging managers to see a Big O as something that should be broken down is insufficient for many of them. They need more help. I encountered this some years ago with a group most of whom readily accepted that they had learned from past experiences, that they could pick out particular experiences of special note, and that it would be a good idea to learn more and learn better. My next step was to ask them to look ahead to some experiences they might be having as managers, and to say which of these could be important learning opportunities. Most of them happily tackled this task, but several sat initially with a puzzled and then a fretful look on their faces. Even looking at their diary did not help them convert from thinking about activities in which they were involved to recognizing them as learning opportunities.

Again in concert with Peter Honey, I have developed a series of exercises which assist managers by spelling out the kind of activities in which they are involved, and from some of which they might learn. My preferred method is to get them to look first at which activities they think they are currently using for learning, and which they might use in future now they have been asked to think about it. An excercise from the *Manual of Learning Opportunities* is reproduced in Fig. 11.3.

Here is a list of opportunities which may have been available to you, and from which you may have learned. *First* use column 1 to indicate which you are already using.

Informal opportunities	Column 1 I am using this for learning now	Column 2 I could use this in future
Stretching the job		
Boss		
Mentor		
Colleagues/peers		
Subordinates		
Network contacts		
Projects		
Familiar tasks		
Unfamiliar tasks		
Task groups		
Problem-solving with colleagues		
Domestic life		
Voluntary work		
Professional groups		
Social committees		
Sporting clubs		
Reading		

Figure 11.3   Future learning opportunities
Source: P. Honey and A. Mumford, *Manual of Learning Opportunities*, Honey, 1989

Formal opportunities	Column 1 I am using this for learning now	Column 2 I could use this in future
Being coached		
Being counselled		
Having a mentor		
Job rotation		
Secondments		
Stretched boundaries		
Special projects		
Committees		
Task groups		
External activities		
Internal courses		
External courses		
Reading		

Summary of column 1

Count up your ticks on column 1 and position yourself on this scale:

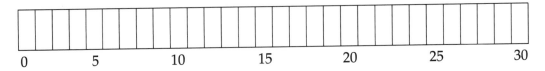

0	5	10	15	20	25	30

I am using a
narrow range of
opportunities

I am using a wide
range of
opportunities

In the light of your score on column 1 items, can you now identify some extra opportunities which you could use in future? Use column 2 to indicate future opportunities.

Figure 11.3   Future learning opportunities (continued)
Source: P. Honey and A. Mumford, *Manual of Learning Opportunities*, Honey, 1989

PART THREE

SHOW ME HOW IT WORKS

Previous chapters have covered first a variety of outputs from cases, and then the structure and background to the design of development activities. Part Three focuses more intensively on implementation. My ideal situation combines a detailed approach to personal development plans (as described in Chapter 4) with a major director development programme (as described in Chapter 3). Chapter 12 describes how individual learning styles were used in a workshop for trainees and in the design of personal development plans, and then in the subsequent director development programme. Chapter 13 describes the application of the philosophy of learning, reality and the focus on real issues identified earlier as prime features of the director development programme. Chapter 14 looks at outputs—what did they learn?

The first part of this chapter draws on my experiences of running learning styles workshops for trainers, developers and educators. The second part shows how learning styles were used in an integrated process of producing personal development plans and running a director development programme for one group of directors.

Learning Styles Workshops

The *Manual of Learning Styles* was first published in 1982, and I ran my first workshop for trainers on learning styles in February 1985 for the National Health Service Training Centre, followed in 1986 by the first workshop open to the general training public. An outline of the workshops which I still run can be found in the *Manual of Learning Styles*.

The workshops consistently provide me with tremendous satisfaction. Unlike many trainers, I am not faced with the potential problems arising from frequently repeating events—I have never run workshops more than four times in any year. The material used in the workshops is practical and useful, and the process is balanced in terms of the learning cycle, and in consequence acceptable overall to nearly all participants.

At the level of rational planning, therefore, I was not surprised by the consistently good feedback—the workshop is designed to ensure that it is experienced as an illustration of the theories and practices proposed. (Like many others, I have experienced events run by trainers which either lack explicit design, or proceed to contradict their own theories.) Nor am I surprised any longer, though I remain pleasantly stroked, by comments about the style in which I run the workshop. 'Relaxed', 'Good at responding to questions', 'Nice touches of humour', 'Good at making us work hard'—I never tire of hearing and reading these, though I never take them for granted. In Australia I received the ultimate compliment: 'They liked you because you are not a pompous pom.'

In addition, I have gradually come to recognize two additional features about the 'Learning Styles' workshop which make it different. The first is consistent through all of them. I am an absolute enthusiast for what I am delivering, and this comes over very clearly to participants. When I am running workshops on 'The Job of a Director' or 'Change', I deliver the content and process well, but I am not an enthusiast in the same way. (By a strange coincidence, while I was writing this chapter I had a telephone call from someone who had been on one of my 'Learning Styles' workshops, who, after telling me how she had used a lot of the ideas and practices contained in it, said 'I am almost as enthusiastic as you are when I put it over to people on my courses.')

The second feature is not always present; it is literally an extraordinary aspect. I do not have to work up my enthusiasm—it is always there. I am not like the politician whose notes read 'Weak point—shout louder and bang the lectern'. Occasionally, however, I move into an even higher gear. I speak with additional power; my voice deepens; my language is precise; ideas and connections flow in a more explicitly effective way even than normal. An example of this occurred at Canberra University in Australia, with a group of academics—not my usual clients for learning styles. I finished the session with an absolute conviction that, above and beyond all the things I had planned for, all the things that had gone as well as they normally do, some extra power had seized hold of me. There was no conscious choice about it at all, it was just an extraordinarily heightened experience. I knew I had had it, although thinking about it afterwards, apart from recalling some of the physical aspects I have just mentioned, I could not actually recall exactly what I had said. The same higher-level experience has also occurred in some of my conference performances, as far apart as London and New York.

The Link

Readers may now be wondering why this section has been included, since this is a book about my experiences with top managers, not trainers. However, it brings out a feature of my work which helps to explain what I do with directors, and may also add something to readers' understanding about the learning organization.

The linking feature is *passion*. I have worked out, through careful reflection from experience, that the learning cycle and learning styles are rational and practically useful tools for more effective learning. An understanding of the learning styles provides the bedrock for improved individual learning behaviour, the absolute prerequisite for improvement in group or organizational learning. The learning cycle not only provides for improved individual learning, but also can be used by groups and organizations as a fundamental discipline. Well delivered, the material makes sense and is accepted by trainers, managers, directors—even university educators.

On top of all that, however, is a passionate conviction. It is the combination of passion and rationality, I believe, that creates such a powerful element in my 'Learning Styles' workshop. I feel that I have a special message to deliver. So when my colleague Joanna said that I was flexible in delivery, so long as my clients were always prepared to accept that they had to do something on learning, she was right. If a group of directors considering asking me to run a major development programme decided that they did not want a workshop on 'Change', I would be surprised and I would certainly debate the issue with them. The debate and discussion would be conducted along (at least on my part) logical and rational grounds. However, if again they were to decide that they did not want to discuss learning at all, and if the same kind of questioning analysis failed to influence their decision, then I would not be willing to run the programme. My fundamental beliefs? My core values? My rational judgement that they could not therefore be really serious about learning and development? All of those to some extent; but at the end, it would come down to my passionate belief that I am right.

So far I have never been faced with this ultimate predicament. I have run one-day sessions on other subjects where issues of learning and learning styles were not priorities and were not included, but I have not yet been faced with the requirement to run a major programme without incorporating the learning cycle and learning styles. Perhaps passion has come into play also in the way in which I present the proposition.

The other point arising from this section is the issue of enthusiasm and passion in relation to the content of a learning organization. I remember the squawk of criticism that met Prime Minister Harold Macmillan years ago when he assured British managers that 'exporting is fun'. I would never offer the generalization that learning is always fun. I *do* say that it can be made far more enjoyable for more people more of the time through the processes described in this book. Passion and enthusiasm can often create enjoyment, fun, all the warmer aspects of the more emotional and less rational aspects of individual personalities and individuals' learning methods. To reach its fullest fulfilment, the learning organization must take on board, in addition to systems, disciplines and rational commitments, the idea that learning within and around work is enjoyable and fun, and is something that can be pursued as vigorously and perhaps as passionately as many other areas of management are pursued by the most effective directors.

CASE 5

Case 5 involved, as was seen in earlier chapters:

- The identification of management issues crucial to this group of directors
- Personal development plans
- The identification of group-wide needs for development
- A subsequent director development programme.

Each director completed the Learning Styles Questionnaire, (LSQ), which was then used as both a stimulus and a constraint. As a positive stimulus, the results were used initially to ask the question, 'Which of these possible activities best fits his or her learning style?' In some cases we were able to go further than this by turning the question 180 degrees: 'Given that he or she has this learning style preference, what kind of activities can we think of which might be attractive to him or her?' While this double-barrelled approach was not achieved in all cases, clearly, the second question tends to generate more possibilities.

The use of LSQ results as a constraint was much more of a single barrel: 'Which of these possibilities is he or she likely to dislike as a potential learning experience?'

Figure 12.1 shows the LSQ results for this group of directors. Statements such as 'Low' or 'Strong' are derived from the norms for the Learning Styles Questionnaire (see the *Manual of Learning Styles*). Our research with directors has shown that as a population they do not learn differently from the general managerial population.

The learning styles material includes a set of statements about the kind of activities associated in terms of preference with a particular learning style. These statements then form the basis of judgement when presented with possible learning opportunities available to an individual; or, as suggested earlier, they provide a way of looking at the preferred

	Activist	Reflector	Theorist	Pragmatist
Green	Moderate	Strong	Very Strong	Very Strong
Brown	Moderate	Very Strong	Strong	Very Strong
Red	Moderate	Strong	Very Strong	Very Strong
Yellow	Strong	Strong	Moderate	Very Strong
White	Strong	Very Low	Low	Very Strong
Black	Moderate	Moderate	Strong	Strong
Blue	Moderate	Moderate	Strong	Very Strong
Pink	Low	Low	Very Strong	Moderate

Figure 12.1   Learning styles results

activities and seeing whether any of them would be suitable for the individual.

Case 5 relates to a real board of directors, not a fictional collection generated to illustrate all the features of individual learning styles. The board members were unusual in that only one individual had a single Strong or Very Strong learning style. This is less than would be expected, certainly in larger groups, because our analysis shows that about 35 per cent of managers have a single Strong or Very Strong score. A second feature was that there was no one with a Low Pragmatist score. A third feature was that the director 'Yellow' had Strong scores for both Activist and Reflector. This is a very unusual and indeed logically a very unlikely combination; it caused further discussion which, again unusually, did not produce a different result.

At the other extreme, four had three Strong or Very Strong preferences, whereas only 20 per cent of our general sample has three Strong preferences.

Chapters 3 and 4 illustrated individual development needs, and indicated how learning style preferences might affect decisions. In *Using Your Learning Styles*, we show 'will learn best from'/'will learn less well from' for each of the styles. Here I have reviewed the styles through specific comments on the individuals shown in Fig. 12.1.

The results indicated in the figure have been merged—Strong and Very Strong results are both called 'Strong', Low and Very Low are both called 'Low'. The extremity of the case indicated by the designation 'Very' is important in giving emphasis to the need to select or avoid a particular kind of learning experience for an individual. However, it does not alter the basic nature of the preference and therefore of the most desired learning solutions.

Illustrations of Learning Styles

Strong Activist (White)

He welcomes the additions to his job and is not disturbed by the uncertainties involved. He enjoys picking up the new tasks and responsibilities. He will acquire some new ideas, but does not think you can plan that sort of thing.

White's enthusiasm will take him into experiences from which he will learn, though he may not do so at the depth that would be ideal. (He has a Very Low Reflector score.)

Low Activist (Pink)

Pink says his worst experiences have been working for a previous boss who roared around stirring things up with no clear plan. He does not like to rush into things unless they have been spelled out, with some sort of structure. (Note also his Very Strong Theorist score.) Pink's Low Activist score matches the demands of his job. He will not be adventurous in pushing for new opportunities, or for taking risks, but his job does not require that.

Strong Reflector (Brown)

Brown says the collection of data has always been fundamental to his approach in his job. The need he expresses to assess the effectiveness of his relationships with his colleagues could be met in part by encouraging him to make notes after significant meetings.

Low Reflector (Pink)

Pink is unlikely to respond favourably to the idea that he could learn from his new activities by keeping a log or reviewing these experiences with his boss.

Strong Theorist (Green)

Green has attended two management courses at different business schools. He says he enjoyed the diversity of experience among faculty and other participants. He rated some of the faculty very highly in terms of intellectual quality.

The ideas suggested on creating a more extensive network of local managerial contacts from other industries, and the suggested books (at the heavy end of the market) should suit him.

Low Theorist (White)

White says he has less interest in concepts and theories on management than about whether something works. (Note also his Very Strong Pragmatist result.)

The need to ensure that his knowledge of manufacturing techniques and standards is up to date is unlikely to be met comfortably through a course or books; hence the suggestion of identifying two or three high-class manufacturers in similar industries which he might visit. He will need help in setting up and planning the visits, and strong encouragement to report on them afterwards. (He is a Very Low Reflector.)

*Strong Pragmatist
(Red)*

Red says he left a course on Managing Time half-way through because he saw no way of being able to apply it in the reality of his job. (Note also his Strong Activist and Very Low Reflector scores.)

In terms of improving his own abilities, the suggestions made here are for one or two short courses run specifically for the industry.

Low Pragmatist

There was no Low Pragmatist in this group. Real life can be awkward sometimes!

However, just to complete the sequence here, if there had been a Low Pragmatist, the comments made would have been that he would not have been worried about whether a development process was geared to the specific current needs of his job and the organization—unlike the Strong Pragmatist (Red) above.

The purpose of this particular chapter is to focus on the use of learning styles, so the full details of the suggestions made in the personal development plans have not been included.

The fact that nearly half the group had three Strong or Very Strong preferences was helpful in two ways. In terms of personal development plans, three Strong preferences indicated the potential to be good all-round learners, and therefore the potential to take advantage of a wide variety of learning opportunities. In addition, there was also a strong potential on the part of these people to be interested at most stages of an off-the-job learning programme, provided it was designed to give appropriate balance to all parts of the learning cycle. These four contrast, for example, with the position of Pink, with his Very Strong Theorist score, who was forecast as less interested in parts of the programme delivered outside his preferred style (a forecast confirmed by subsequent events—see Chapter 6).

Use of Learning Styles on the Director Development Programme

Throughout this book, the proposition has been that the learning process is fundamental, and that it has to be overt and to be constantly visited and revisited during the programme. It should however be remembered that the prime overall purpose of the director development programme is not to show that it could be designed through the learning cycle: the cycle was a means to an end—but if you do not get the means right, you will not reach the desired end.

In fact, I planned to use the learning cycle and learning styles in three ways:

1. As a means of controlling both the general design of the programme, and the specific learning styles contained within the group
2. As a vehicle for developing 'Learning to Learn' concepts and techniques and thereby improving the capacity of participants and learners
3. As a means of continuing discussion on, and perhaps increasing the implementation of, personal development plans

The design structure for the linked series of five workshops described in the next chapter involved these directors in working on their real issues and problems. Around those problems, they were provided with the opportunity to generate their own insights, and to add to their knowledge through various forms of tutorial, input or reading. Within that overall structure, the learning cycle was used both as an objective and as a check.

The objective was that, during any day of the workshop, participants would experience all four stages of the learning cycle. While the greater emphasis was on the stages of reviewing, concluding and planning, the experiencing stage was covered also, since the participants were working on real problems. The experiencing stage was also a substantial contributor to the reviewing stage, since participants were often responding to variants of the question, 'What has been our experience on this issue so far in our business?'

In practice, the workshops constantly encountered a familiar problem. The planning stage was always at risk of being underplayed or postponed until after the workshop—'We need to work on the problem a bit more.' This was particularly true for the workshop on Strategy, where the intensity of work and the area to be covered was simply too much for a two-day workshop.

As already indicated, the small number of Low learning style preferences meant that there was unlikely to be acute antagonism to any stage of the learning cycle among the group as a whole. Other groups with which I have worked have presented a different picture. Sometimes there are fewer all-round learners, which increases the chances of individuals being less attracted to particular stages of the cycle. The workshop in case 1 illustrated the opposite experience, of working with a group dominated by a Strong Theorist learning style preference.

Learning to Learn

The programme was also explicitly designed to assist participants not only to understand better the nature of the learning process during the workshop, but also to develop their capacity to learn outside the workshop.

There are two strategies of response to learning styles results, once they have been accepted as valid. As has been indicated through the examples drawn from personal development plans earlier in this chapter, the most practicable strategy for most people on most occasions is to go with the flow. The grander title for this is to choose a 'congruent' strategy, i.e. to choose development solutions that relate to Strong preferences, and avoid those related to Low preferences. On this programme, it was possible to give attention to the second strategy, which involved helping participants to make better use of their existing strengths, and to take some steps to improve their ability in their Moderate or Low learning styles.

Early in the first workshop I ran a session in which the meaning of the learning cycle and learning styles was presented and discussed, and then the proposed application throughout the programme was illustrated. Not incidentally, the learning cycle was used to design this session. So individuals were asked to look at their past learning experiences, then at their experiences so far on the workshop; they reviewed their LSQ results and discussed the validity; then they were asked to draw conclusions. Strongs and Lows were agreed (as they usually are).

Participants were given the opportunity to work on this through the personal workbook *Using Your Learning Styles*. Each chose some aspect on which they would work, and shared ideas on this with fellow-members of the programme. While most achieved this, at least in terms of writing something down and discussing it on the programme, it had less impact than I had hoped. Although this particular workbook was added to their personal development plans, and raised for discussion at each workshop, in practice discussion gradually faded away. This was a failure on my part, since I did not allow sufficient specific time for the exercise, or provide ways in which the commitments they had undertaken—for example to make better use of a style or develop one on which they were low—could be discussed and improved.

In a second session, participants were introduced to the idea of a learning review, supported by a learning log or learning diary. Learning reviews continued throughout the programme. They covered two different areas of ground. First, participants were asked in each succeeding workshop to discuss what they had done with what they had learned from the previous workshop, and what they were doing to meet any learning objectives set for themselves as individuals. As already explained, these learning objectives could have been contained in their personal development plans, could have been added to their personal development plans through the first workshop, or could have constituted the special features of building their learning styles preferences. A second version of the learning review was a task set, usually around the middle of the afternoon, on 'What have we learned from the workshop so far?'

On this programme I used for the first time a process for learning reviews which I should have thought of before. On previous occasions, this had been a solo personal and private exercise in order to emphasize the potential for really intimate soul-searching analysis and plans. This time the learning reviews were conducted mainly in pairs, sometimes in groups of four. With the agreement of the participants, the pairs were chosen as far as possible on the basis of Strong opposites. (On this programme I made the choice in advance, whereas on Learning Styles workshops I get the participants to identify how we should choose the pairs and to choose them themselves.) For example, White (Strong Activist/Very Low Reflector) worked with Green (Moderate Activist/Strong Reflector). Because of the number of people with three Strong preferences, this allocation by difference might seem less significant in this group than in some others. In fact, however, in relation to the Learning Review process itself, there were significant differences which could be used both as illustration and in development.

There were four Strong or Very Strong Reflectors who could be paired with two Low and two Moderate Reflectors. The Strong Reflectors would be predicted to find more value in the learning review and even in the learning log. This was indeed largely the case. Feedback from the pairs confirmed that the Low and Moderate Reflectors got more out of the learning review process in pairs than they did when they undertook this as individuals at the beginning of the first workshop.

The suggestions made on keeping a learning log were much less effective. Some of them did keep notes in between workshops, but at nothing like the level of review and reflection that a learning log is intended to encourage, and which indeed the guidance note I gave them showed. Again, this was in large measure my fault. With four Strong Reflectors, there was a substantial body of participants who should have needed relatively little encouragement to keep learning logs because it would have been in tune with their preferred learning styles. The design in this area was too informal and relaxed. Participants should have been asked to tackle both the learning log and the learning review sessions more seriously; they should have been set explicit written tasks; the time set aside for it should have been longer; participants should have been required to share notes on a much more purposive basis. It really required me to provide the time and direction on each workshop for each individual to keep a learning log and conduct a learning review, and to put at least one public comment into the open session.

Personal Development Plans and the Learning Styles Workshop

It was my expectation that the workshop would provide an opportunity for individuals to review progress on the PDPs agreed before the workshop started. This was in fact designed into and achieved on the first workshop, but it was not really successful. Participants had discussed the personal development plans in brief with their bosses and were not so willing to discuss the same issue with their peers. In addition, they felt that the PDPs had been a useful process, but not one that had high priority in terms of the group issues they were trying to tackle on the workshop. Their view, with which I concurred in designing subsequent workshops, was that the PDPs could and should be discussed outside the workshop context. The problem here was that the chief executive, who had been very keen on the initial process, had been less active in actually agreeing to and following through the plans.

Passion is not Enough

I started this section by talking about my passionate commitment to the subject of learning, of learning to learn, the learning cycle and learning styles. So strong is my conviction that all my substantial programmes include this subject. Yet my review of this particular programme shows that my passion was not always accompanied by appropriate techniques or, to be brutal to myself, real commitment on some aspects of what was required. My sessions explaining the learning cycle and learning styles are delivered with an enthusiasm and panache that brings nearly everyone along with me. But thereafter, in the reality of the kind of workshops I run dealing with real issues and problems, there is a clash between attention to learning and working on the problems.

In this case, the directors became very committed themselves to working on Strategy, Change and other issues. Since, after all, the whole programme was based on the premiss that these are the things on which they need to work and which turned them on, there is no surprise that they are not equally dedicated to working on learning issues. The dilemma is that, even if I do insist on providing more and more explicit time for attention to learning issues, which I know in myself to be the right thing, my clients will not recognize the same priority. In this programme I was insufficiently assertive (or, more bluntly, too cowardly) to confront them with the issue and to get them to see why they should allocate what was after all only going to be another 30 minutes in a two-day workshop to the issue. The increased time and attention I gave on this programme, compared with that in case 4, was still not enough.

| **Do Participants Really Behave Like That?** | It has been one of my interests to observe participants on a programme to see how far their behaviours match the predictions that have been made as a result of their learning styles results. |

White did indeed struggle with any of the sessions involving analysis of information, and found it very difficult to do a learning log or learning review. Yellow had managed to score himself as both a Strong Activist and a Strong Reflector, and had stuck to this when I suggested that he revisit the Questionnaire. He was consistently late in arriving on the workshop days, always with some other priority which had overtaken him on the way to the workshop—predictable for a Strong Activist. The chief executive had insisted that telephones should be taken out of our workroom, and that all messages were taken in a separate room, but Yellow brought his portable telephone with him. Although he avoided the chief executive's wrath by switching it off during the general open sessions, he frequently used it not only during breaks, but when he and others were supposedly working in pairs or groups.

Since his behaviour was not positively disabling to the rest of the group, I decided not to intervene and watched with some interest and subsequent amusement to see what would happen. During one of the workshops he went out of the room. Later when he attempted to use his mobile phone in the way described above, it did not work. He did everything to make it work except bang it on the table, not noticing the smiles and giggles around him. At lunchtime as we began to break up, one of his colleagues said, 'Oh [Yellow], have you found out what is wrong with your phone yet?' 'No, the damn thing still isn't working.' The giggles now became more obvious, and he realized something was going on. 'Do you think it's because of this?' said one of his colleagues, holding up the batteries that he had removed from the phone. Nothing else was said, but Yellow never used the phone in our workroom again.

The Achievement of Integration

The process described here not only enabled dual use of the LSQ, but also provided the opportunity to integrate understanding and working on more effective learning processes for the individuals involved. Valuable as the LSQ would have been for either personal development plans or the general programme, it became even more formidably useful when employed in these two linked development activities.

Two further benefits emerged from the level of integration that was achieved. First, there was explicit attention to 'learning to learn'. Individuals were enabled to understand their own learning on the programme by declaring and reviewing the learning processes in which they were involved. It still seems to be one of the great lost opportunities of any formal programme that it does not use the opportunity to enable participants to discuss how they learn, and how their improved knowledge about their learning might be employed away from the programme.

The second major benefit of explicit attention to learning issues, using the shared yardstick of the LSQ, is that this group of directors came to understand itself and its individual participants better. They saw each other's relative strengths and weaknesses as individuals, and began to make use of those strengths in some of their group processes.

A third benefit was that participants also saw that the knowledge they had gained about how they learned could be valuable in their work as superiors of other managers. This enabled us to discuss, in the final workshop on Selection and Development, the need to manage any differences in learning preferences between bosses and mentors.

More Situations and Cases

As is shown in detail in *How Managers Can Develop Managers*, mutual knowledge of the learning cycle and learning styles leads to a more productive developmental relationship between one manager and another. The desirable position, of course, is that these 'Helpers' (see Fig. 12.2) should ensure that individuals are going round the Learning Cycle by checking out that each individual is actually giving appropriate attention to each stage.

Boss
Grand boss
Mentor
Colleagues
Subordinates
Project client/sponsors

Figure 12.2   The six helpers
Source: A. Mumford, *How Managers Can Develop Managers*, Gower, 1993

In relation both to giving appropriate emphasis to each stage of the Learning Cycle, and to recognizing and using learning opportunities, the learning style of the Helper has a major influence on what the Helper actually does. Helpers will tend to identify learning opportunities congruent with their own preferred learning style, and will assume that the individual they are trying to help will learn from the same opportunity in the same way. Where there are opposite Strong or Low preferences, there will often be less achieved learning than frustration.

Understanding of each other's learning styles is extremely helpful in developing more effective one-to-one relationships. It can substantially reduce the irritation that individuals otherwise feel about each other, for example as the Strong Theorist develops not just one but several 'big pictures', while the Strong Pragmatist, low on Theorist behaviour, wriggles uncomfortably and wishes they could focus on the particular problem under discussion.

In the direct work situation, I have found in groups that the learning styles information has generally been used more, and more explicitly, than has the learning cycle. The board of a company I was working with actually retained the flipchart showing their scores in their boardroom for a couple of months to remind themselves not only of their scores but of some of the actions they had promised to each other to make more effective use of each other's strengths.

I had an earlier experience in which group members did not know each other's scores, but where the chairman's recognition of his own Strong and Low preferences became important both for his learning and for his management of the group. He was a newly appointed British divisional chairman who had taken over a number of companies, including some from the Continent. When I was working with him on his personal development plan, he commented to me that he was finding it difficult to learn as much as he needed to about these companies because, particularly in management meetings, he found that his new colleagues were not offering much in the way of suggestions about their own or other people's activities. As a result, he claimed, he was having to take all the decisions on his own shoulders.

This man's LSQ scores showed that he was a Strong Activist, and further discussion of the situation he had described showed that as a Strong Activist he was rushing into action without developing the questions necessary to draw information out from others. He was struck both by his Low Reflector score and by the fact his meetings really did not satisfactorily encourage the review stage of the learning cycle. Together, we developed some behaviours that would increase his Reflector style—and he told me afterwards that in subsequent meetings he had drawn far more out of the participants. It would of course have been interesting to know the scores of the rest of the group!

Five Additional Characteristics

The learning cycle and learning styles provide a model for the design of learning experiences. Important though that is, even more is to be gained through the insistent deployment of the model and of data derived from it in enabling individuals to learn to learn. More important still is the ability of the model and the diagnostic instrument to provide characteristics additionally facilitative of learning. These five characteristics are shown in Fig. 12.3.

- *Consistency* of learning cycle with more familiar task cycle
- *Continuity* of learning through both on-the-job and off-the-job experiences
- *Co-operativeness* between individuals through greater knowledge of learning cycle and learning styles
- *Correlativeness* between preferred learning style and choice of learning opportunity
- *Courage* in developing additional learning skills

Figure 12.3   Characteristics facilitated by the learning cycle and learning styles

13 A Director Development Programme

The organization described as case 5 in Chapters 2 and 3 proceeded to implement a Director Development Programme. The proposed sequence of workshops was agreed with no trouble, although there was a little more difficulty in agreeing dates. While I experienced some frustration with getting a decision at various stages, once the decision was made, I was fortunate that the chief executive's new personal assistant became a very important ally. She got the dates agreed, identified and managed the relationship with the hotel where we ran the workshops, sent out papers, books and preparatory material to participants. Apart from her efficiency, one of the additional aspects of her involvement, which I realize fully only in retrospect, was that she was in the chief executive's office, not in the personnel office. I believe this was helpful not because the new personnel director, who joined before the programme started, was as unenthusiastic as his predecessor, but simply because she was able to speak with greater authority than the personnel director's assistant could have done.

I have made *this* point first, rather than the more obviously important issues of content that follow below, for two reasons. First, without dates and a location, there is no programme. Second, administrative detail is not one of my strong points. Planning this programme at a macro level, in the sense of overall design, sequence and discussions with tutors, I am good at; remembering to check that we have two flipcharts in every room and the right numbers booked for lunch, can easily escape my memory.

The General Design

The programme comprised six workshops, each with a major theme as described in more detail below. The original timetable for the whole programme was that it would start in July and finish in February of the following year. In fact, the second workshop was postponed to the date of the third workshop and the remaining workshops were similarly shifted. We then had a series of rearranged but postponed dates until the final workshop was held 14 months after the start-up workshop, instead of 8 months as planned. As a half-full-glass person I was delighted they wanted to finish the programme—if I had been a half-empty-glass person, I would have been even more frustrated than I was at the succession of postponements. These postponements occurred because of a clash with completion dates on one of the company's main projects, and the reasons for postponement were not trivial, but once again I was in the position of pressing for a decision—or concealing my frustration by being pleasant when I was told that they had to postpone again.

The overall design for the programme was that there was a single major theme for each two-day workshop, but half of one of these days was spent discussing progress either on the individual projects, or on major issues that had been taken up by the board itself during and subsequent to a previous workshop. Most of the work was done in the full group of eight directors, but occasionally they were broken into two groups of four—and for learning review and personal development purposes into pairs as described in the previous chapter.

Examples of Projects

The projects were all proposed at workshop 1. Examples included:

- Producing a business plan for Technical Services Division
- Producing proposals for handling price variations with a contract
- Producing a proposal for a new product line

The projects all met the criterion of being things that were of significance, on which the individual held prime accountability, and on which the programme in effect was providing the stimulus for 'something we have been meaning to tackle for some time'. Compared with other organizations and other projects I have been involved with, the weakness here was the failure to identify a client or clients, and insufficient attention to the way in which individuals were carrying out their projects. For example, they were not required to produce a project statement or plan for agreement with their client—even though the notes I gave them on effective projects had emphasized exactly that point.

I chose the tutors for each workshop. This was not negotiated with the client. However, each tutor visited the organization, and had specific discussions with one of the directors about the workshop for which the tutor was responsible. Apart from the overt purpose of collecting material, of course, the tutor visits gave the tutors some closer contact with at least one individual director prior to the programme—and in some cases with several. This was part of the design to ensure that the content of the workshop was tailored as closely as possible to the particular needs of the organization.

It was not necessary or desirable to design case studies, but it was extremely important to identify the most important issues that should be discussed. After the visit, each tutor drew up a list of questions that participants should think about before coming on the workshop, and recommended any articles or books that ought to accompany the workshop.

The Programme Themes

The chief executive and I had some discussions about the most relevant sequence of workshop themes. The sequence we chose placed Strategy as the second workshop, in preference to for example, Change or Teamwork, because the organization actually needed to refine and develop its strategy as quickly as possible.

The following summaries show what was included in each workshop.

Workshop 1: The Job of a Director

This aimed to look at the difference between corporate and functional roles, at directing the future and not just managing the present, and of the differences in this particular organization between being a senior manager and being a director.

In addition, we planned to look at individual and group learning processes (choosing groups and pairs to distribute learning style preferences—see Chapter 12). Finally, we wanted to work on setting up and managing individual projects for each member of the board.

Workshop 2: Creating a Strategy and Business Plan

This organization had a partial business plan, but had no fully developed strategy. The purpose of the workshop was to provide first an analysis of where they were—the familiar SWOT (Strengths, Weaknesses, Opportunities, Threats) analysis—and then of where they wanted to go to. In one-and-a-half days they would not succeed in drawing up a complete strategy, but they did identify the major elements on which they agreed to work, on an additional day they set themselves.

We also planned to review progress on individual projects.

Workshop 3:
Teamwork and
Creativity

This organization had already used the Margerison–McCann Questionnaire for identifying team roles. However, so far this had been used only as a part of the selection process for board appointments, and for rumination by the chief executive. It was now to be used as the major part of the workshop on the reality of participants' team roles, on how these worked together, and on how this information could be used to generate more effective teamwork. In addition, they would discuss how information about team role preferences could be used in, for example, setting up projects with managers below them.

The actual composition of team role preferences is shown in Fig. 13.1.

	Major	Related
Black	Explorer/Promoter	Creator/Innovator, Assessor/Developer
Brown	Creator/Innovator	Thruster/Organizer, Explorer/Promoter
Red	Thruster/Organizer	Concluder/Producer, Assessor/Developer
Yellow	Assessor/Developer	Explorer/Promoter, Creator/Innovator
White	Assessor/Developer	Thruster/Organizer, Concluder/Producer
Green	Thruster/Organizer	Assessor/Developer, Creator/Innovator
Blue	Thruster/Organizer	Assessor/Developer, Concluder/Producer
Pink	Concluder/Producer	Thruster/Organizer, Controller/Inspector

Figure 13.1   Team management preferences on Margerison–McCann instrument

Workshop 4:
Directing Change

In principle, the idea of having established what directors should do, and having drawn up the outline of their new strategy and prospective changes, and the different kinds of contribution they would be expected to make within the team, led neatly to this workshop. The logic was more than somewhat weakened by the gap between the workshops—this one took place five months after the Strategy workshop.

Workshop 5:
Selection,
Development and the
Organizational
Context

The major thrust of this workshop was to take up some of the ideas discussed in workshop 1 about learning and development, to continue their application to the directors themselves, and then to see how they could carry them through in personal dealing with their subordinates. In addition, the workshop was aimed at actually examining the plans for development of the next level of management, and especially at developing people for newly defined organizational roles of general management. Finally, the workshop was to discuss candidates for both general manager jobs and longer-term succession to the board.

Workshop 6: Review Day

This was the half-day workshop referred to in Chapter 6. It was run on site four months after workshop 5.

Preparatory Work

Since the philosophy behind the design was the integration of the programme into real work, and of real work into the programme, participants were asked to think about their actual work situations before each workshop. They were also given a small amount of reading to do.

The preparatory work for workshop 1 was:

1. Please prepare a five-minute presentation on your views on:
   (a) the difference between being a manager and being a director.
   (b) any major constraints you feel inhibit you from operating as a Director.
2. Complete and bring with you the enclosed Managerial Roles Questionnaire.
3. Read Chapter 8 of Mumford, *Developing Top Managers*.
4. The programme gives you an opportunity to work on a problem, opportunity or project. Come prepared to discuss what you want to do; you may have several alternatives. Your issue may be individual, shared with one or more others, or a proposal for the top team as a whole.
5. Read the attached 'Note on choosing a problem/opportunity/project'.
6. Review and bring with you your Personal Development Plan, Learning Styles Questionnaire and Learning Diagnostic Questionnaire.
7. Re-read Alan Mumford's report, 'Management Development for the Board', and bring it with you.
8. Identify some personal objectives you have for your participation in the programme, and be prepared to discuss at least one of these.

Other workshops also involved preparation. For the Change workshop this was:

1. Read Chapters 1, 3, 5, 6 in Rosabeth Kanter's *The Change Masters*. (Many of you will find the remainder of the book also well worth reading.)
2. Prepare to discuss the following questions:

    (a) From Chapter 1, given her definitions, how orientated to change is this organization?

    (b) From Chapter 3, review her 'Ten rules for stifling innovation'. Have any of these applied in this organization recently?

    (c) From Chapter 5, what are the change motivators in this organization?

    (d) In Chapter 6, which of these suggestions are most important for effective implementation of your project?

The Workshops in Action

Case 5 provided the major benefit of a complete board, which meant that we could work on real problems and issues for a group rather than a collection of individuals. In that sense, we were prospectively a lot closer to organizational learning. However, some additional problems were brought into the programme which we had not expected. As the notes below show, I felt differently about this at different times. As the director of the programme, I wanted it to stay close to objectives and to the unique opportunity to look in detail at issues the board would not otherwise look at. As an action learner and a realist, I could see the case for taking up issues outside the programme if they were genuinely of high priority.

Workshop 1: Job of a Director

We started only five minutes late. One director was missing, dealing with a major contract. When he arrived he said that the board had to make a decision in the next two days on the pricing for the contract. There was some discussion on whether this decision could be made after the programme finished at 6 p.m., but this turned out not to be viable. So we had a $1\frac{1}{2}$-hour break while the board discussed the contract, and made its decision.

When the directors returned, I led a discussion on what they had done, how they had done it and how this related to their earlier discussions on their roles as directors.

Day 2 went very well. They spent most of the day in pairs or as a complete board looking at action plans arising from their discussions of the previous day.

We spent less time than I had planned on reviewing progress on their personal development plans, and also less time on the proposed projects—ideas about which had in some cases been changed by the discussion of the previous day.

We did spend the 30 minutes I wanted on a learning review. The range of comments was fascinating:

- There was less theoretical input than I expected, but it was probably right.
- Make sure we have the capacity to type up the flipcharts.
- Was working in pairs and in groups better than all of us together?
- [The chief executive] I feel very good about the two days. We dealt with important issues which are crucial to the business. It is also true that I am on the hook for a lot of what we need to do.

Workshop 2: Strategy   Everyone turned up on time for this. They worked hard at the SWOT analysis. They finished with some clear conclusions about what they need to do—unfortunately, some of these were things they ought to have decided three years earlier.

They liked the tutor I chose for this—his experience in industry and his general style went over well. We deliberately played down any big books and alternative models, in favour of actually getting participants to work hard on things that they could recognize.

We had a fascinating discussion about the board and the executive. There was a lot of dissatisfaction about what was discussed at board meetings, where, when and how. The discussion grew out of one of the projects that one of the participants had taken on, and it then became a big issue. They asked me to chair a discussion on this, which I happily did, and they began to reach some conclusions. The problems were familiar—too much attention to operational detail, papers not delivered in advance, insufficient time for thinking ahead. 'We should not need this programme, helpful though it is to do some of the sensible things we are now doing.'

Workshop 3: Team Management   We started this workshop by reviewing the project for an hour, instead of spending two hours on it the second afternoon. As usual things went slowly. I suspected they had not fully taken on board how seriously the projects were meant to be pushed.

Starting with the project reviews was deliberate, because we thought this would lead into issues of who was doing what in terms of work preferences and then on to the team point. It seemed to the tutor and myself that it would be helpful to start from this point rather than diving straight into the team analysis.

I also found that the chief executive expected me to run the discussion on this point. I had let this happen the previous time, but this time I explicitly moved out of this role. I said these were their projects to meet their own purposes; I was merely providing an occasion, through the workshop, when they could discuss progress together. I talked to the chief executive about my concerns over this. He said everyone was terribly busy but that it was a good thing that they could be reminded of their commitment through these workshops.

The team management profile information went over extremely well. As usual, participants were fascinated by their own scores and those of their colleagues. They recognized the difficulties they were encountering as a team because of the imbalance towards Thrusters/Organizers, with only one Explorer/Promoter.

They liked the tutor. I had had no concerns about using her, although they are an all-male board in an industry totally dominated at all management levels by men. I was not surprised by the feedback—'she is very clear and strong'.

There was another interruption to deal with a pressing issue. I felt that this one was less necessary, but of course, once an immediately important point gets raised, the possibility of avoiding discussion on it is very low. The chief executive did, however, limit the time allowed for the interruption.

Workshop 4: Change

I had written to the chief executive after the previous workshop commenting that the gap of three months between workshops would be likely to reduce pressure on the participants to carry through their actions on all the issues we had identified so far, and especially the projects. I suggested that he and I meet to discuss how things were going, and we did so. We talked about his own role, his views on the programme so far, and his own personal development plan.

The Change workshop itself went well. There were some rueful comments about the fact they needed this earlier, in view of changes they had made. There was some unexpected feedback on the Rosabeth Kanter book, of which I am a great fan. They had been asked to read several chapters of this. Some of them found this 'very hard going'. The chief executive said that it was literally hard to read because I had chosen the paperback version (for cheapness): 'Use the hardback, so we can read it easily.'

Workshop 5: Selecting and Developing Key Executives

We finally met for this workshop on the third date that had been arranged. From my point of view, we covered the planned ground very well. The balance between looking at themselves as individuals and then looking at how they would help others to develop was good. The fact that they were working on a lot of tasks was something most of them enjoyed, though a couple of them were a bit uncomfortable with the personal analysis.

We got into one major area of difficulty in the task I had agreed with the chief executive on establishing the criteria by which they would select high-flyers. The fact that they needed common criteria was usefully established, but the actual lists were extraordinarily different.

One bit of good news was that 'Yellow', who had missed most of the first workshop, and had frequently brought in problems and tasks to do 'in the breaks', attended this one full time with practically no outside involvement.

Learning Reviews

I set three different kinds of learning reviews during the programme.

The first version was:

1. Look back at the last workshop ... and consider your personal learning, the content of your Learning Log, and what you put on your Learning Opportunities Review.
2. What have you done on these?
3. What additional points are there to add from this workshop?
4. Consider any revisions necessary to your overall Personal Development Plan—what will you do before the next workshop?

Another example shows how a learning review can be brought into the middle of a workshop, in which participants are asked what they have learned today about:

1. The distinction between strategy and business plans
2. What this organization needs to decide in order to define its strategy
3. What actions you might personally undertake or suggest
4. What actions others might undertake or suggest
5. What particular points or emphasis you want to suggest we cover tomorrow

A third example asked:

1. What are the main points you have learned today?
2. What insights from previous workshops affect how you

need to direct change (Job of a Director, and Role of the Board; Strategy and Business Plan; Team Roles)?

3. Identify crucial points from this review for discussion in the next plenary session at 4 p.m.

Integration

Figure 13.2 sets out ideas on some of the things that need to be done to integrate work and learning.

Interaction	—with colleagues plus boss, mentors
Implementation	—accountabilities not consultancy
Integration	—off-the-job design to aid on the job
Iteration	—continuous learning through conscious use of further opportunities.

Figure 13.2   The four I's in work-centred learning
Source: A. Mumford, 'Learning in Action', *Personnel Management*, July 1991

In many ways, this programme provided both the greatest test and the greatest achievement against these statements. This was a real team working together on common issues through the real relationships between boss, subordinates and colleagues. The accountability was clearly with the board itself—they were not consultancy projects undertaken for someone else. The learning process was made explicit; the Learning Cycle was addressed both in design and implementation at each workshop. Connections were made between learning on the workshops, application on the workshops and implementation on the job.

Results of Learning Reviews

The learning reviews during the workshops were, the participants and I felt, both helpful and effective. The links between workshops, personal development plans and action in between workshops was nothing like as satisfactory—I simply did not give sufficient emphasis to this side of things.

Projects

Achievement on projects was also much less satisfactory than had been achieved on other director development programmes. I failed on some aspects: for example, thinking through who the client was for the individual projects—the chief executive for all seven other than his own? The board as a whole? In what sense could the board be the client? Only about half the participants actually completed their projects. I was interested to see from my notes how many interventions I made to try to return ownership of the projects to the individuals and to the chief executive, without success. The problem was really a much bigger one, of the relationship between the chief executive and the other directors in terms of clarity of goals and monitoring of performance. This applied throughout and not just to projects.

My Roles

Revans's statement about the teacher's 'inveterate hankering to be the centre of attention' has been a favourite of mine, and I have therefore put myself last in this chapter. I had five roles:

1. Designer of programme
2. Programme director
3. Tutor
4. Constant presence
5. Counsellor to chief executive

My role as designer has been described. I was the single tutor for workshops 1 and 5. As programme director, I selected tutors for the other three workshops, explained to them what I wanted, arranged for them to visit the organization and then discussed their proposed content for their workshop. In my role as 'constant presence', I was able to observe them in action and to collect feedback from them.

As 'constant presence' I attended the three workshops on which I was not the lead tutor. This was agreed with the client because we felt it would help to ensure that the successive workshops were integrated. It was indeed the case that I was able to suggest linking points, both in advance and during the workshops. For example, in the Team workshop I was able to help by relating some of their discussion to the decisions they had made about the relationship between board and executive and the kind of commitments they were seeking from each other. I was also able to insert learning reviews by direct intervention (with the agreement of the tutor for the workshop). This ensured that they took place, following an earlier experience where a tutor had agreed to build in learning reviews but had not in fact done them, because of the pressure of content for 'his subject'.

Clearly, the chief executive was my main client and I deliberately and explicitly focused additional attention on him. I occasionally inserted what I thought to be balancing questions or issues when attention in the public sessions seemed to focus unduly on what he had done or not done, compared with his colleagues. More privately, I worked with him on his own personal development plan and learning reviews. His colleagues accepted this as quite natural. In addition, he would talk to me about the content of the workshop, how things were going, how issues at work related to what we were doing. I would occasionally suggest to him things that he could point out or ask for in subsequent sessions on the workshops.

I enjoyed all five of these roles. Although I have been critical earlier in this chapter of some failures on my part and on theirs, overall there was a tremendous feeling of satisfaction, on the part of myself and the majority of the Board, on the progress made.

Implications for a Learning Organization

One of the encouraging features as we went through the workshops was that, whereas at the beginning I would have to remind participants about the learning cycle and why we were doing learning reviews, by the third workshop they were able to articulate the learning cycle themselves when I stopped the action and asked them what we had been doing so far and what we should now do. So they had taken the process on board in terms of the programme. Sadly, I had less success in trying to get them to tell me how far they were applying the learning cycle to their normal work as a board, though some individuals told me they were doing so. They needed a chief executive who was not only convinced by the idea (as this one was) but who also had the mental discipline to push it through into his board and executive meetings. This chief executive in some aspects of his managerial style was not very disciplined and systematic. Without that direct encouragement, the board probably needed some additional external intervention to follow up and encourage them to introduce the task cycle/learning cycle idea into their normal working practices.

The action that individuals took on their personal development plans, and the use they made of learning styles, also varied considerably. Some did take in the idea and used it at least during the period of the programme, although, again, I have no information on what happened afterwards.

One particularly fascinating point returns us to the potential for integrated learning offered by a board of directors as compared with a group of directors from different organizations. The immensely powerful process of working on real problems, the real concerns and issues raised for discussion, produced at times the pungent smell of explosions during the workshops. There were some personal conflicts, some of them longstanding, that were raised. These were not really resolved, but more effective action was taken on some aspects of how one director related to another, how one director worked with the chief executive. Basing our work on real-life situations, in my view and in theirs too, produced much greater returns than some of them had expected and than some had experienced on other management training programmes.

The number of interruptions to several of the workshops showed organizational reality overcoming the priority of working on development and longer-term issues. I felt protective about 'my programme' and would have preferred that the chief executive had not allowed, or on one occasion precipitated, interruptions to the planned day. On the other hand, the particular reasons were always good, and were not the sort which I could say simply represented their over-dedication to the detail of the present. My conclusion now is that the risk of interruptions of this kind is a price you pay for working with a real board in real time. In many ways, it represents the reality of the learning organization, because it shows how difficult it is actually to stick to an explicit learning process even when you are away from your normal work-place.

14 Learning for the Learning Organization

Chapter 6 described what individuals and groups had learned from the projects and programmes described in Chapters 1–5. This chapter sets out to look at achieved learning from the more specific perspective of things learned which were of special relevance to the learning organization.

Process Consultancy Cases

Cases 2 and 8 were primarily about diagnosing, giving feedback on and assisting changes in management style and methods; case 1 involved the same kind of activities, then led on to workshop activities. Until the workshop phase in this latter case, none of these projects had involved learning and development as explicit objectives on the part of either the clients or myself. They were seen as ways of gathering data, and then of communicating the data. The data added to the knowledge of the managers and directors involved, and to their understanding and perception of the problems. In that sense those involved learned something. Inasmuch as a learning organization is often thought to be about the stimulation of ideas, the open sharing of information, the creative identification of and final adoption of ideas for improvement, they might be claimed as organizational learning projects. Indeed, I see claims of that kind made for projects that look very similar.

I do not, however, claim the above cases to be organizational learning projects. They contributed to organizational learning because of the characteristics just mentioned, but they fail my own definition because they were not geared to explicit objectives about learning. 'The behaviours and practices' encouraged through the projects contributed to learning; but the participants learned how to *manage* more effectively, rather than adopting behaviours and practices which enabled them to *learn* more effectively.

This test seems to me a fundamental one. Otherwise we are

in the position of saying that any form of learning contributes to organizational learning, which leaves us with a definition of and understanding about the significant processes contributing to organizational learning far below that necessary to make reality of the phrase.

The projects could all have been made into more overt and effective contributors to organizational learning. The proviso would have to have been that the client agreed to this extension of objectives. In at least one case not reviewed in this book, I had a client who did not want such an extension. He wanted help on his own role, he wanted to discuss ongoing problems, and later he wanted clarification of the role of his board and his management committee. He was not willing to agree to an extension of these basic consultancy activities to include how he and his colleagues were learning from the process of being helped. Because I included in the project a review process with him, he was very happy to discuss what help he had actually been given, but he was not willing to see this reviewing process as part of a learning cycle.

These three cases illustrate the provision of data and feedback from an objective source. They exemplify the creation of special opportunities to review the data, to reach conclusions on it and to plan the next steps. Managers would have recognized these words as creating the task cycle. They recognized in all of these cases the virtues of additional data and of the dedicated review process. In equivalent cases now, I would be more aware of the opportunity to provide a double-value exercise involving learning as an explicit element.

The Research for 'Making Experience Count'

The point has been made earlier that all our research has shown that directors (like managers) are unaware of the ways in which they have learned, and of what they have learned. It is precisely because of this lack of awareness that many of them became turned on by our interviews, and why in my workshop experience with directors on learning they are interested and prepared to review how they learned.

Generally, therefore, the contribution of this research has been to show that directors lack the capacity to create a learning organization, since they are not familiar with, let alone skilled in, the behaviours and practices necessary for effective learning. There were just the occasional gems gleaming in the information we collected, as shown in Chapter 9, pages 111–119.

The lack of full consciousness about what has been learned raises the general question of transferability of learning. Usually this term has been applied to the transfer of learning from a course to the real-work situation, and this aspect will be discussed further below. In the context of this research, however, we looked at the even more fundamental issue of whether individuals transferred learning from one kind of work experience to a different working situation. Our research, using the four approaches analysis, showed that 75 per cent of the 'hindsight' experiences had application beyond the original and particular situation. Unfortunately, this does not show us whether the transfer was appropriate. It is of course possible for individuals to learn the wrong lesson, or to learn the right lesson but apply it in the wrong situation, or to learn the right lesson and apply it in the right situation but in the wrong way. I have always been fond of a quotation from Plato: 'Experience teaches our best fluteplayers. It also teaches our worst fluteplayers.'

Learning from Difficulty

Participants in the research have been unaware of their learning processes and of opportunities for learning. They have developed knowledge about how to handle learning from difficulty, and perhaps have gained some insights about it and some skill; e.g.:

'You do not always see the difficulty and the potential to learn from it.'
'I did not see the learning at the time—I saw it later.'
'It is really discussing it with you and thinking about your questions that has brought out both why the situation was difficult and what I learned from it.'

Again, a few had learned something about learning:

'Reflection leads to understanding which leads in turn to the discovery of meaning.'
'Although it requires courage, asking for support from competent people pays off.'
'I had a boss who would never acknowledge failure—so mistakes were repeated.'
'Learning for me is what I can generalize—maybe because I like systems and models.'
'The lessons I learned on introducing quality assurance I applied when I was moved to developing a project strategy.'
'Basically, the learning is specific at the time and you generalize it later.'

Unfortunately, not all learning seems on the face of it helpful to a learning organization:

'The only learning on which you can generalize is people.'
'Never admit failure to anyone who has power.'
'Don't trust anyone else.'

One of the main, though not unexpected, findings of this research was how unhelpful organizations in general, and bosses in particular, are in enabling individuals to learn from difficulties, problems and failures. What most individuals had learned was not to expect any help on the problem, let alone to learn from it. This is of course the exact opposite of what a learning organization should provide.

Director Development Programmes

Statements by participants about what they have learned and used which are particularly relevant to my ideas on organizational learning include:

'I've used learning styles in allocating projects and discussing Personal Development.'
'I've learned to listen. This not only helps develop others as well as myself, but I never knew how powerful silence is.'
'I used the exercise and checklist you gave us on the programme to discuss the results of sales visits with my people. I asked them, 'What have we learned from this visit?'
'I think more and reflect as a result—which changes the actions I would have taken.'
'I thought I knew about managing a project. I knew less than I thought I did, and I certainly found out from this programme how to learn while managing a project.'
'I had never thought about the learning process before. I understand myself and other people a lot better in this area.'
'Learning reviews were an excellent feature—you could spend more time on them.'
'My boss did not really understand what the programme was about—he thought it was another straightforward training event.'
'Neither the personnel director nor the managing director was as involved as they should have been. They should have talked to me more about it.'

Developing Others

Although in most of my director programmes there has been a final workshop under some title such as 'Developing Others', on which the issue of carrying through their own learning to help others learn has been addressed, the final learning review has probably not given sufficient attention to this. From an organizational learning point of view, however, the point is the need to give every possible emphasis to the issues of continuous learning beyond this splendid but isolated experience of the director development programme.

Case 7 was particularly important in relation to this point. Here was a workshop specifically designed to help senior managers and directors assist others in their learning. The specific statements made by participants on this included:

> 'I have already planned how to identify better some real-work experiences to develop my subordinates.'
> 'I am going to develop a workshop on similar lines for discussion with the whole of my management team.'
> 'It was fascinating to see from the examples we produced ourselves here how much more there is to learn from our normal work.'
> 'Four of us are involved with a significant project and we can design learning experiences from and around it now.'
> 'I had always known that individuals are different—now I have a way of finding out how they might approach a learning experience.'

What Kind of Learning?

One way of appraising the kind of learning that people have secured is shown in the following questions:

- Is the learning unique to this particular problem or situation?
- Is the learning generalizable from this problem or situation?

One of the problems with many development programmes, particularly from business schools, has been that they have worked through the reverse process; i.e., they have assumed generalizable learning and hoped that people would apply it in specific situations. The kind of work described in this book has operated entirely the other way round. Not least because of the work-focused process, learning has generally been experienced as specific and situational, but has then been, at least for some participants, generalized. Unfortunately, this has not always been achieved, which indeed is what could be predicted for example by weaknesses in the reflecting and concluding stages of the learning cycle.

It may also be the case that my programmes have given insufficient emphasis to asking people to generalize from specifics. Generalizing different situations in order to be able to apply to new problems is obviously tremendously important in organizational learning, which is likely, in any event when successful, to generate more new situations. So the application of a specific skill of listening generated through programme experience is, as one of the comments made above shows, situationally created through the programme but generalizable to that director's work situation. The same can be said of the comment made earlier about not only managing a project but learning from managing a project.

I avoid the error of conducting programmes that ask participants to find their own way of implementing generalized skills and knowledge in their specific situation. However, my emphasis on the specifically situationally valuable learning from action learning programmes has not provided sufficient opportunity for individuals to generalize beyond the particular experience.

Beyond this specific compared with generalized learning, there are issues about different levels of learning, about different kinds of learning as exemplified in discussions about differences between learning and development, and about incremental or transformational learning. I am familiar with the relevant material—Bateson, Saljo, Pedler, Argyris. However, their concepts have not so far influenced the way in which I approach defining what people have learned.

Some Less Satisfying Experiences

Nearly all my work has met with approval at the level of immediate participant belief, and in those cases where I have done follow-up reviews there have been reasonably convincing statements about continued application. As I have confessed, ironically, the area in which I have the least comfortable feeling concerns the issues of carrying through learning processes—by yet another Mumford paradox, precisely the area with which I am personally most emotionally involved.

Not all my work, however, has followed a seamless path neatly moving from diagnosis to successfully achieved action. Nor has all of it been satisfying to me, even though the client was satisfied.

CASE 10

A public sector business, due to be privatized in six months' time, had been working with a firm of management consultants on a variety of issues for the previous six months. The consultants had identified and worked on middle-management training needs, but the chief executive decided that he wanted a different individual to work with himself and his top team on development needs. The organizational structure involved a board with a part-time non-executive chairman on which sat the chief executive and three other members of his executive staff. The executive staff had an additional three members and excluded the chairman. The management consultants brought me in, and I met the chief executive.

The main issues on which he wanted help were help in identifying the development needs of himself and his senior managers ('the executive'), assistance in carrying out appraisal of these senior managers and help in drafting his own self-appraisal for discussion with his chairman. (I met the chairman over lunch; he asked, 'Where do you practise your black arts?')

It was agreed that I would review existing appraisals and other material available from the management consultants, and would interview each of the chief executive's colleagues as the main means of identifying skill requirements. I would discuss the general process he was using and would sit in on one appraisal and give him feedback. As far as his own appraisal was concerned, I would talk through the issues involved for a chief executive being appraised by the chairman (which had not previously happened), and would then take him through the process before he actually saw the chairman. Following this, there would be an early one-day workshop in which the results of the interviews would be discussed and some initial work would be done on clarifying the roles and skills. This in turn would lead to further workshops.

The most frequently mentioned issues in the individual interviews were:

• The need to find time for the longer term, and for bigger issues
• The fact that their regular executive meeting was seen as too much concerned with detailed management rather than with longer-term direction
• The pace of change
• Time pressures

The most frequently mentioned skill requirements were:

• Leadership
• Taking a corporate rather than a functional view
• Strategy
• Team skills

There was an interesting balance between positive and concerned views about the impact of privatization; cultural change was recognized as inevitable, but this was balanced by the expected release of creativity and energy upon being changed from a public-sector to a private company.

They were also asked to identify what they saw as the special issues involved in moving into the private sector:

• A commercial profit-making business orientation
• Relationships with the City
• Understanding legal liabilities
• Speed of response to the market
• Interrelationships on the board

The transition from public to private sector involved significant differences in the skills and knowledge required. The executive had not been able to turn itself into an effective team in management terms, let alone to turn itself into a learning team. This is one situation in which the idea that learning often may involve transformational rather than incremental learning would clearly apply. Indeed, there was clear awareness, among all the members of the executive, that their skills and knowledge would have to be enhanced for them to be effective as a private company. They might have balked at the idea of continually transforming themselves, as suggested in the definition of the learning organization by Pedler and his colleagues, but they showed themselves in subsequent workshops to be interested in the idea of continued learning.

Compared with other cases, the time-scale is also interesting. Discussion with the chief executive on his own 'self-appraisal', and sitting in on the appraisal with one of his senior managers and reviewing it with him immediately afterwards, took two months to arrange. The full set of interviews ocurred one month later. The first workshop took place five months after the first interview with the chief executive.

The workshop combined a discussion of the issues raised by the interviews and discussions about the new skills required of the people who would become directors in the new organization. In addition, we looked at some of the behaviours in this team, at learning processes and at the different roles of directors and managers.

The chief executive was pleased with the day, and asked me to submit a proposal for further workshops based on the priorities they had identified during this first interaction. Since quite a lot of discussion at the first workshop had identified major pressures on their time, my proposal was for three separate workshops covering four days altogether. After discussion with his colleagues, the chief executive replied that he thought the proposal was a bit expensive in both time and cost, and asked for two one-day workshops. His colleagues also turned down the idea of taking on a significant project, either as individuals or as a team, on the grounds that they had too much work already.

I ran the two one-day workshops and we managed quite a bit of integration of their ongoing issues about how they managed themselves as a team and their priorities; we also brought to the surface some issues about the relationships of individual executive members and the chief executive. I introduced a session on 'networking', and it became clearer that one of the problems in and around the executive was a relatively high-wall type of management, in which different divisions and functions really did not interact effectively.

I produced for them copies of flipcharts and lists of actions they had agreed to undertake, and these were fed at least partially into their normal executive meetings and processes.

I had carried out a good diagnostic process, had engaged the complete executive in discussing the issues they needed to work on. We had worked on a number of these issues, and had added a significant additional topic to their original recognition. The feedback to me from most participants, and particularly from the chief executive, was complimentary. So why does case 10 appear in this chapter? Why is my judgement, that this was an unsatisfactory experience, different from theirs?

Since I have claimed myself to be a half-full-glass person rather than a half-empty-glass person, I should say that this was a half-success rather than a half-failure. In my view, we simply did not spend enough time on the issues we did cover, and we left out some that we should have covered. I made a mistake, which in some degree is a continuing temptation for me, of trying to squeeze too much into a workshop. In this case, I knew very well that I was being asked to cover too much, and was not tough enough in either asking for more time, or in cutting out more of the material.

In one sense, the executive was to be congratulated on giving any time at all to working on these issues and on their own development at a period when they were under intense pressure. Their unwillingness to spend more time was I think much more a realistic view of their own situation than any kind of implied comment on the relevance and value of the work I was doing with them. However, I accepted an impossible target in trying to deliver too much over the two one-day workshops, because I was intrigued by the organizational problems they faced, keen to help them overcome the problems, and particularly keen to help the chief executive, who had opened himself out to me in a way unique among the chief executives with whom I had worked up to that time. I also thought that if I did these workshops they would in the end come back for more. They never did, which therefore reinforced my feeling of dissatisfaction that I had not done a deep enough job on the issues we did discuss.

That is my feeling, not the clients', but I did set myself for the future a firm rule that I would not be persuaded, or persuade myself, to try and pack in too much material. In addition to what it says about me, this case says something about the pressures on an organization which genuinely may wish to give emphasis for the first time to the development of its top team. This executive needed to improve its skills to manage the transition to the private sector and to direct the organization in the future. Its needs were clearly identified and accepted. It allocated more time than had ever been provided before (none) for the development of its top people. Yet an organization which in some senses needed to transform itself found it difficult actually to agree the time necessary to direct the transformation successfully.

I had finished the final workshop by saying that I would follow up some three months later to see how they were progressing on the actions and behaviours they had agreed. However, I had not proposed a formal meeting—a mistake I have commented on in earlier chapters. I wrote to the chief executive, who replied saying that the workshops had been valuable, that they were pursuing a number of actions arising from them, but that it was the wrong time to consider further development activities.

CASE 11

The managing partner of a professional organization asked me to come and see him to discuss the possibility of a management development programme. They had only recently begun to understand that their management capability was well below their achieved professionalism. He wanted to do something about it, and asked if I would design a development programme for the senior people who were carrying management responsibilities.

I replied that, although I was obviously happy to take that on as a longer-term objective, any development programme ought to be based on a clear understanding of what their management responsibilities actually were. So I would not offer to design a management development programme for them, but would instead offer to discuss with his senior colleagues what their managerial responsibilities were, what the skills involved were, and what might be done. He and his colleagues on the Management Committee accepted this idea, and I proceeded to interview them. As a result of these interviews, I presented a report to them which first reviewed their own concerns about management as a process and their individual participation in it, and then offered my own suggestions on what might be done.

One of my main conclusions was that they had absolutely no management culture at all—management was a task you took on as an obligation because your colleagues wanted you to, not something you undertook as itself a desirable or satisfying activity. As several of them put it to me, while they were managing they were not earning fees for the firm. There was no clarity on what any of those carrying managerial responsibilities were expected to achieve, let alone how they should achieve it. Nor was there a proper remit for the Management Committee—the clearest thing was how it was elected, and a negative statement about what it should not do.

My report was accepted as an accurate and helpful analysis, and it was agreed I should proceed to a further stage, still not providing a management development programme. I returned to the interview trail with a slightly wider remit in which I interviewed additional people outside the Management Committee, looked at potential structures and relationships, and elicited the terms of reference for the chairman of the Management Committee and for people carrying out specific large functional responsibilities. I produced terms of reference for the Management Committee and job descriptions for each of the main job holders and members of the Management Committee. Individual participants all agreed their job descriptions, and commented that they were necessary and useful. There was still uncertainty among a number of them about whether as individuals they wanted to carry the managerial responsibilities which they now saw ought to be exercised by someone.

My report was submitted, but discussion was delayed. Then it was delayed further. Finally, it was postponed for a major management meeting, which then became associated with activities by another consultant on other aspects of the organization and its work. The chairman of the Management Committee who had been my initial and prime client had passed over responsibility for this work to one of his colleagues, and my letters and telephone calls to that colleague produced no response.

The organization involved had had two reports from me, which a large number of its members had apparently valued (and for which they had paid very promptly). I do not know if they implemented the recommendations on the Management Committee and on individual job descriptions contained in my second report—I suspect not, because otherwise they would have called me in for clarification and discussion. Perhaps the whole concept of clarifying responsibilities setting objectives for the Management Committee was something so culturally alien that in the end, despite earlier protestations, they could not come to terms with such a process. However, I knew from discussions in competitor organizations that some of these were much more clear about management processes than this organization—indeed, some of my interviewees had worked for such organizations and missed the clarity of management they had had before. I believe I listened hard for any messages that might have told me that stage 2, where I worked on these issues of structure and responsibilities, was too far away from what they might be interested to pursue. With the exception of one or two individuals who were not, in fact, apparently particularly politically powerful in the organization, the majority seemed to want clarity and structure.

I have included this case for two reasons. My work provided this organization with an opportunity to look at itself, to review its successes and failures and the destination it wanted to take in terms of managing its own future. There was considerable enthusiasm for taking up this process. Yet what I may have helped them to manage was only one half of what they needed to do. They now knew much more about their management practices and some detailed steps necessary to change themselves from the kind of organization they had been to the one that the majority of them wanted to be. I was not successful in engaging them clearly in the action phase—unless the good I did lived after me and they carried on without my help!

I could have designed a management development programme taking up the specific issues of managing effectively in a professional organization, and picking out the skills and knowledge that they would need. I am sure, from comments made to me early in my discussions in the organization, that such a programme would have been accepted—a couple of them had been on external management courses and liked the idea of a programme specifically focused on their own organization. However, what I wanted to do was to build the programme as I saw it on more appropriate foundations, starting from clarity on the managerial work they would do rather than initially on the skills they needed to do it.

I could have provided a management development programme that would have looked good, felt good and received pleasant feedback from the majority of participants. But I would never have been sure that it was 100 per cent relevant to their needs. Perhaps my view of the 'best' answer drove out a quite decent 'good' answer. I might have finished with a more satisfied client—and could have earned the same or more money from them in fees—if I had run a development programme. But I felt at the time, and still feel, that what I gave them was what I knew as a professional they should be offered. In that sense, in so far as I have some feeling that this project was not fully successful, it feels to me a partial failure of which I can be relatively proud.

Summary

Both of the above cases seem to me to represent something of significance, not only in helping to improve my own approach to work, but in identifying issues about the learning organization. Those who seek to stimulate the learning organization from outside need to repeat for themselves a familiar mantra:

1. What is the situation in which I am being asked to help?
2. Who recognizes what problems?
3. Who is the client?
4. Am I offering my solution to the organization's problems— or offering my solution to the problems to which I have solutions?
5. One more time, who is the client?

PART FOUR

HELPING ORGANIZATIONAL LEARNING

This part of the book looks first at the people involved in facilitating organizational learning, and then at the features of my own contribution, before finally summarizing some of the main themes of the book.

16 Managers Develop Themselves—and Others

**Self-
development—
Not Once but
Always**

The learning organization starts with the individual. Unless individuals are learning, there can be no learning organization. The danger of some businesses that are beginning to describe themselves as learning organizations is that they have become overexcited by the possibilities of learning as a total organizational process.

Thus, we need to emphasize again, as was initially done in the early proposals on self-development in the 1970s, that:

1. Individuals decide *what* they will learn.
2. They also decide *how* they will learn—or at least whether they will reject a particular method of learning.

Illustrations have been given earlier of the integration of individual learning processes, derived through personal development plans or director development programmes, with continued learning on and through the job. Personal development plans of course represent much of the most focused effort to provide an analysis of needs, and potential solutions, that are appropriate to a particular individual (although not necessarily to another). Director development programmes by their nature deal more with general needs for the particular group, so additional emphasis and attention is required to enable individuals to recognize, through learning logs and learning reviews, the items that have most relevance to them as individuals.

A group of anything from 8 to 16 directors cannot have individual one-and-a-half hour interviews. Instead, they review their own needs. They start with some review of their past learning experiences, and then move on to an exercise setting out a variety of learning opportunities (see Fig. 11.3).

Note: The opportunities identified here are not necessarily separate. You may for example think of something first in terms of it happening at a meeting—or you may think of the way in which one of your colleagues achieved success at a meeting.

Situations within your organization
Meetings
Task—familiar
     —unfamiliar
Task force
Customer visit
Visit to plant/office
Managing a change
Social occasions
Foreign travel
Acquisitions/mergers
Closing something down
Starting something new

Situations outside your organization
Voluntary work
Domestic life
Industry committee
Professional meetings
Sports club

Processes
Coaching
Counselling
Listening
Modelling
Problem-solving
Observing
Questioning
Reading
Negotiating
Mentoring
Public speaking
Reviewing/auditing
Clarifying responsibilities
Walking the floor
Visioning
Strategic planning
Problem diagnosis
Decision-making
Selling

People
Grand boss
Boss
Mentor
Network contacts
Colleagues
Consultants
Subordinates
Project/task force clients

Figure 16.1   Learning opportunities at work
Source: P. Honey and A. Mumford, *Manual of Learning Opportunities*, Honey, 1989

Another exercise, focusing in more detail on opportunities around the job, is shown in Fig. 16.1. Again, it will be noted that we progress from managerial activity, which managers readily recognize, to the understanding of managerial activity as a learning opportunity. Once they can recognize it as a learning opportunity, individuals can be asked to consider how they can most effectively take advantage of it. In order to illustrate this process, I introduce another exercise:

Turning Experience into Learning

1. Select one activity from the Learning Opportunities Review which was especially important to you at some time in the last two weeks.
2. Review what was involved, why it was important to you, and what you believe you learned from it.
3. Consider what you now think you learned from it in the context of the other processes we have considered on this workshop (e.g. the learning cycle and learning styles).
4. What conclusions do you now draw?
5. What plans will you make for learning even more effectively from such an activity in the future?

Of the four approaches this is a Retrospective learning exercise. Individuals can be asked to consider the same list and identify an opportunity that may be occurring within the reasonably close future and to predict how they will learn from it—the Prospective approach.

All these exercises are built round the use of the task cycle, learning cycle and learning styles, though the sequence in which these three devices and learning opportunities are discussed varies according to the needs of participants and the consequent design of the programme or workshop.

Self First, Others Later

My director development programmes often include 'Developing other Managers' as part of the content. Participants are asked to use the same ideas as those used in the development exercises above.

Some of my work is carried out in workshops devoted solely to issues in self-development, for which my general workshop title is 'Developing Ourselves as Managers'. In addition, I run workshops with the general title 'Managers Developing Managers'. Sometimes the two are combined in one workshop, in which case the movement from developing yourself to developing others is an integrated feature of the workshop. If the workshop is focused explicitly on managers developing other managers, then it is still based on the essential principles of understanding your own development processes before you engage in trying to develop anyone else. Before undertaking the task of reviewing the development needs, development opportunities and the development processes involved in developing someone else, it is vital that managers understand themselves.

Managers Who Help Learning

My research and my experiences on development programmes over the last ten years have given another thrust to my work. In the course of this research I asked directors which individuals had been helpful in their development. I was especially interested in the contribution of boss, mentor, peers, subordinates and networkers.

A few directors had been substantially influenced by bosses and mentors, but often in their very early days rather than recently. Formal management development policies setting out the responsibilities of bosses, even where such policies existed, had apparently had little impact. Nor had the majority of directors had experiences they recognized as being facilitated by a mentor. (I distinguished between the roles of boss and mentor—different individuals with different managerial relationships.)

It became increasingly clear to me, looking at my own work and that of my colleagues in my business school, which focused on development through action learning, that we had given insufficient emphasis to one of the major contextual factors—the people surrounding participants at work. I began to develop some material to assist in discussion of and work on the kind of help that should be provided on the job by the managers involved. This in turn led to workshops and then to my book, *How Managers Can Develop Managers*.

That book describes, with lots of exercises, the situations that provide opportunities for one manager to help another, the processes through which this can be done and the nature of the helping relationship. For the purposes of the present book, it would be redundant to repeat all that detail. The important question here is, what features are crucial in contributing to the development of a learning organization?

Figure 16.2 sets out the line management relationships.

Boss
Grand boss
Mentor
Colleagues
Subordinates
Project client/sponsors

Figure 16.2   The six helpers
Source: A. Mumford, *How Managers Can Develop Managers*, Gower, 1993

Many readers of this book will themselves be consultants or advisers on management development—or as I expect to see any day now, someone with a title of 'organizational learning consultant'. They are missing from Fig. 16.2. The reason of course is that I have carefully defined the figure to cover only those with a direct line relationship. (In another book, *Management Development: Strategies for Action*, I have included development specialists, since the book is written with a different perspective.) As a development specialist myself, it may seem perverse that I have left such people off the chart. However, I want especially to focus on line managerial relationships because they are so crucial in understanding what is required for the development of the learning organization.

What Do the Line Developers Do?

Since writing the book mentioned above, I have identified more clearly the sequence of contribution which I think line managers may offer in facilitating the development of others. This sequence is set out in Fig. 16.3.

1. Opportunities	Enabling others to recognize the opportunities for learning that exist, especially at work
2. Process	Enabling others to understand and use effective processes for learning, e.g. task cycle, learning cycle, learning styles
3. Skills	Offering developmental help through the appropriate and effective deployment of skills, e.g. listening, coaching, problem solving

Figure 16.3   Sequence of development help

The three features of this sequence represent not only different requirements for the line manager, but a hierarchy of difficulty. With the kind of help offered through my book or workshops, the identification of learning opportunities is the easiest (though not easy) of the steps. At one level managers do this already—though it is what I have described as 'Big O'. The next step—learning processes—is more difficult, because most managers have no understanding of this until they are exposed to some description and personal work on what is actually involved. The third step—skills in helping—is by far the most difficult.

Skills—the Most Difficult Area

We now come to a paradox—yet another in the Mumford Encyclopaedia of Paradoxes. Formal management development has tended to concentrate on equipping managers with skills. Twenty years ago, formal training in coaching skills began to be provided. More recently, progressive organizations have gone in for mentoring skills. Both are extremely desirable skills—as indeed is an even wider range if one manager is to help another. The paradox seems to me to be that this is by far the most difficult area in which to work, for two reasons. The courses imply that, and are often delivered as if, coaching and mentoring were required purely as management development skills, and they start from a management development proposition. That is to start from the wrong point. Very few managers actually have any experience themselves of either coaching or mentoring, or of being coached and mentored. While this of course has been the reason for the argument that they should be developing these skills, we have in the past failed to understand properly the managerial context and managerial motivation. Managers do not think of coaching, and rarely experience it. What they think about and experience is problem-solving. Here is an example:

> A boss arrives at a subordinate's office at 8:30 on Tuesday morning. 'I have been thinking about that problem with Client Y you raised with me. I think it might mean not just a specific problem of that kind, but something that runs across several clients. Why don't we get together for two hours on Friday, review what the issues are and how we might tackle them?'

The point here is that neither the manager nor the subordinate would in the normal managerial context think that what was going to happen was 'coaching'. The problem with a great deal of what has been attempted in formal management development systems is that establishment of the development process has been attempted on a separate managerial activity called 'coaching'. In consequence, we have often been developing, with the best of intentions, skills about which managers may be temporarily enthusiastic while on a workshop, but which they often will not deploy subsequently because they do not recognize the situations as appropriate to coaching. Or, they may return from the workshop and actually set up specific sessions called 'coaching'—which in the end seem unrealistic to both parties.

So the first problem about the undue focus on the development of skills lies in the inherent lack of reality in and commitment to the process by the managers involved. The second problem is that the skills involved require managers to behave towards each other in a way that is foreign to their normal managerial behaviour. Desirable as it obviously is that managers should develop excellent listening skills in order to be effective coaches, this is a requirement for most managers in most situations, not just for coaching. Unless their listening skills can be developed for application in the much wider and more realistic managerial context, emphasis on listening skills for coaching purposes will not survive very long. This is not an argument for not developing listening skills—merely a comment about the likelihood of doing so solely in a coaching context.

The conclusion I have drawn from this analysis has been that it is likely to be much more effective to give emphasis to steps 1 and 2 in Fig. 16.3. So the time I devote on my workshops and similar activities is proportionally devoted more to steps 1 and 2 than to attempts to develop skills.

More on the Learning Hierarchy

Progress towards organizational learning happens most effectively through a series of learning relationships, as illustrated in the learning hierarchy in Chapter 11. The first relationship is internal—within individual herself or himself—an understanding of methods of thinking and working and how these are carried out in pursuing learning opportunities.

The second relationship is between individuals and the people surrounding them. Managerially, these are the individuals identified in Fig. 16.2 and the extended version of it, which includes consultants, advisers, network contacts and domestic partners. These relationships can be immensely powerful and productive, and sometimes they are at work. They can be made more conscious and purposive in the context of development programmes—see earlier illustrations of paired learning reviews, work on learning opportunities, discussion of learning logs.

While compared with twenty years ago there is now a volume of experience, understanding and literature on these first two types of relationship, there is as yet remarkably little on how individuals learn in groups. Oddly, perhaps, what there is is available at two extremes. One is the construction of groups on relatively traditional management training activities, discussing case studies or doing exercises; the other is represented by T-groups and their descendants, in which participants at least look at their interactive processes though all too rarely at the way in which they learn. With these exceptions, there is very little to guide us on what actually happens within groups as learning vehicles. This is a major area for analysis, experiment and discovery, because not only would improved understanding and skills lead to more effective use of opportunities in groups, but such work would provide the necessary final steps towards the learning organization. (See Karen Warkins and Victoria Marsick, *Sculpting the Learning Organization*, Jossey Bass, 1993, for some thoughtful work on this.)

Even in action learning, which provides so much of a focus for and statement about the powerful nature of the group as a situation and vehicle for learning, relatively little has been written. All the writers on action learning agree that action learning sets provide a marvellous opportunity for individuals to learn with and from each other—but we have little written evidence about how they actually do it.

Finally, we come to the learning organization. I have prefigured the point here in earlier chapters. Unless you get the first three sets of relationships to work effectively, organizational learning will be a rhetorical goal rather than an organizational achievement.

Last and Least Important?

The reason why this chapter would concern itself with line managerial relationships was emphasized early in this chapter. There may seem an inconsistency in writing a book that will be read mainly by professional advisers which then gives no direct tribute to, or statement about, the role of advisers in bringing about the learning organization.

One reason for this is that I wanted to emphasize that the central character in organizational learning, since it will be focused on real work, must inevitably be the line manager as helper. One way of declaring our sincerity of purpose when we say that we want to enable managers themselves to take more responsibility for development is to emphasize that declaration by concentrating solely on the line manager's role.

Another reason is that in my previous two books (*Management Development: Strategies for Action*, IPM, 2nd Edition, 1993 and *How Managers Can Develop Managers*, Gower, 1993) I have written quite a lot about what advisers should and should not do.

The third and probably most powerful reason is implied in the design and content of this book. It is a review of my personal experiences in attempting to bring about worthwhile management development processes. I said at the beginning that I would not be calling for support from other people whose experiences and methods of work are similar to my own. Nor is this an academic book where I would contrast my methods with others who work in a different way. For this book, the relevant issue is not what advisers in general might do, but what this particular adviser actually has done, and why. Some elements of the 'why' have been revealed as we have gone through the chapters so far. Now we turn to a more detailed and, indeed, more intimate review of why I make the contribution I do.

17 A Not So Brief Note About Myself

My work involves asking my clients to say a lot about themselves, often focusing on their strengths and relative weaknesses. This chapter turns the question round the other way, and shows particular personal features affecting my contribution to the learning organization.

I was once described in the United States as a learnerholic. Like the psychiatrist's patient who saw sex in every picture shown to him, I see learning possibilities everywhere. This chapter is not an ego trip, but an attempt to explain why I work the way I do, and to learn more about myself through the explanation.

When dealing directly with clients, or to assist someone chairing me at a conference, I provide a CV, which I generally describe as 'A Brief Note about Myself' (Fig. 17.1).

ALAN MUMFORD
Specialist in Director and Management Development
BA, D.Litt.

Alan Mumford's experience in management development has been exceptionally wide. It included periods with John Laing & Sons, IPC Magazines, International Computers Ltd and the Chloride Group. He was also Deputy Chief Training Adviser at the Department of Employment.

In 1983 he was appointed Professor of Management Development at International Management Centres, and is now Visiting Professor there. His main work is on improving management performance, especially through effective learning processes. He has worked with senior managers and directors and developers in a variety of organizations including Ford of Europe, Pilkington, Brooke Bond and Unison (the UK's largest trade union). He has worked with organizations in Australia, South Africa and the United States.

He has published numerous articles and books on management development including:

The Manual of Learning Styles (Honey, 3rd ed, 1992)
The Manual of Learning Opportunities (Honey, 1989)
Developing Top Managers (Gower, 1988).
Management Development: Strategies for Action (IPM, 2nd ed, 1993)
How Managers Can Develop Managers (Gower, 1993)

Figure 17.1   'A brief note about myself'

Sometimes at conferences I am asked to provide some more personal facts. I then mention my wife, who has her own career in social work, and my two daughters, both university graduates just entering the world of work at the time of writing this book. If I am pressed into even more personal revelations, I mention a great love of cricket and the theatre, and that I am a collector of political cartoons in a variety of forms. If I am confident of the company I am in, or am prepared to accept the abuse that goes with the confession, I add that I am a supporter of Arsenal Football Club.

The short note says nothing about the way I work, nor about the reasons why I work in the way I do.

Before Work

The first equivalent of an appraisal that I received was a school report which said that I had 'the ambition to be the buffoon of the class, and shows every sign of succeeding.'

I did National Service in the Royal Army Educational Corps, which helped to provide me with experience relevant to my subsequent career. It also provided me with enough experience of outdoor manoeuvres for me not to feel it necessary to pursue this kind of activity in my later management training career.

I read and enjoyed history at Cambridge and developed a significant feeling of self-worth through two achievements: I did well in my degree, and I participated in the debating society and in the Labour Club of which I was chairman. Through this latter interest I developed the capacity to speak effectively to large groups, often much more unruly than any I have encountered subsequently.

The study of history helped to make me what I am (while of course recognizing that the kind of person I was helped me to choose the study of history). I recently came across a comment by Professor G. R. Elton, whose performances in the lecture theatre I much admired at the time. He said that the study of history is directed to 'a sharpening of the critical analytical faculty, and a deepening of the imaginative and constructive faculty'. A. J. P Taylor's observation is also relevant, that we learn nothing from history except the infinite variety of people.

Diagnostic Information

I did David Kolb's Learning Styles Inventory again recently, and emerged as an Assimilator, resulting from my highest scores being on Abstract Conceptualization and Reflective Observation.

The Honey–Mumford Learning Styles Questionnaire shows me as a Very Strong Reflector, and a Very Low Activist. I was only a Moderate Theorist—a difference from the Kolb result. There might be some question about how accurate an answer to my own questionnaire can be—except that all the feedback I have ever received about my own behaviour confirms it.

Other Information from Work Situations

My involvement with management training began at John Laing. I had the good fortune to work for Don Stradling, who set high standards and reviewed against them. He was also excellent at other aspects of development, especially at providing me with additional opportunities to learn, even to the extent of giving up work he enjoyed himself. Among many items of helpful feedback, one had a significant influence on me. He told me that the power of my intellect got in the way of my warmth. I have tried to correct the balance. In work relationships and on courses, I have hoped to create a sense of pleasure and fun, by the use of humour. Many people enjoy this, but it may be an unduly limited contribution to 'warmth'.

Feedback over the following years as an internal management development adviser, business school professor, and now as an independent consultant has remained consistent. Psychological tests say the same. I am seen, and see myself as, reflective; analytical; relatively cautious rather than adventurous; determined once I know what I want to achieve; articulate on my feet and clear in written communication.

I chair meetings very well; I am good at checking out actions and plans. I am usually described as a very good listener—but I recognize limitations on what I actually hear, because of constraints on the questions I ask.

Other Feedback

Feedback from Courses I Have Attended

I had useful experiences on courses at Ashridge Management College, including a four-week General Management Course. My achievement on that course of producing the largest loss ever recorded by a company on a business game I decided to treat as an objective experience, and did not use it at that time as a reason for not running business games.

More powerful experiences later included a Coverdale Course, and a Shephard Moscow Consulting Skills Course. Coverdale was especially useful because it provided a structure for understanding 'task' and 'process' which I did not then have. I asked all the other members of the team I was in to take it, and we subsequently developed our use of the ideas very effectively in our work. This was a major illustration to me of the additional power a group or team can have in learning and applying learning together. Shephard Moscow was even more powerfully illuminating to me, because it gave immediate and direct feedback on some aspects of personal skills. One observer commented that I very much set my stall out to be liked. Another commented later in the week that, as my interaction with someone else had demonstrated, 'you can't be acceptable to everybody'.

I have been less persuaded by courses with a substantially emotional direction or content. For example, I disliked being blindfolded as a means to learning about trust.

Feedback from Participants

I do not provide evaluation sheets on my own courses. I ask direct questions in private of my main client, and also pursue feedback from, for example, a management development adviser who may have initiated the project. I am probably not as good as I should be in pursuing more, and more detailed, feedback. In terms of my own performance, I feel this is due to the fact that I tend to be working with relatively small groups with whom I spend a lot of time and whose reactions I observe very carefully and note in my personal review. The comments I get again say much the same thing consistently— 'Good at listening to what we want to discuss', 'Helps us to focus on the most important issues', 'Sensitive at recognizing what is going on in the group', 'Good at establishing connections'.

Feedback from Colleagues

I carry out a lot of my work solo. While in some respects I am very comfortable with this, I actually seek opportunities to work with others. Although we have worked together on programmes very rarely, Peter Honey has been a major influence on my work quite apart from the learning materials we have written together. Graham Robinson has been especially helpful on the two director projects, and actually provided the description 'Integrated' for the type 2 learning described in my Model of Management Development (see page 106). I have worked with Jonathan Coates, and admire his fizz and energy. More recently I have worked with two consultants, Patricia Hodgins and Claire Breeze, both of whom have major strengths in areas in which I feel much less capable—particularly issues of personal values and emotions. The general virtue of working with colleagues is that I can discuss content and process with them, and ask for explicit feedback. They tend to confirm my strengths already listed.

I Am Not So Effective at ...

My first reaction to any work situation in which I am involved is analytical, rational, with a strong concern for collecting data before reaching conclusions. In many ways I am the epitome of the Reflector.

The other side of these strengths is that I have to think my way into looking at feelings, emotions and personal values as issues, rather than immediately identifying and responding to them. I recognize three reasons for this:

1. I do not talk about my own emotions and feelings much, and have probably persuaded myself (through rational thought, of course) that if *I* do not want to delve into my own feelings much, I should not ask others to.
2. I usually feel myself faced with priorities about what should be discussed. Again, no doubt, my own priorities take me to the view that it is sensible to focus on the more directly discussable management issues, behaviours and style rather than on the more concealed issues of personal emotions and values.
3. This is an area in which I certainly lack intellectual arrogance. I often feel the likely inadequacy of comments or help I might offer on emotions and feelings, and on any interpretation I might be asked to offer. (It is true that otherwise in my work I am unlike Churchill's description of Attlee—a modest little man with plenty to be modest about.)

A good illustration of this is the exercise I give to managers on 'Past Experiences of Learning'. When I set this exercise, I always qualify it by saying I want people to record, with a view to subsequent discussion, their managerial or professional experiences (while allowing them to record, of course, some things even in those areas that they would not want to discuss). Before adopting this constraint, I encountered an individual who had been through a most difficult experience in his personal life. His most significant learning experience was 'going through a divorce'. Neither I nor the other participants in the workshop could really cope successfully with the fifteen minutes over which he reviewed this experience. It was extremely important to him, but not something that I felt able to handle in a way that was helpful to him. Nor could I or the participants successfully 'convert' this experience into one that we could 'use' on the workshop.

These are not, however, areas in which clients ask me for more. Perhaps some clients choose me because of the strengths they see from our early discussions. Perhaps some others do not ask me to work with them because they see from discussions that I will not take them into the areas of emotions and values.

Managerial Experience

My first client in case 2 had strongly dismissive views about personnel consultants who had never been managers as he saw it. He asked me early in our relationship whether I had ever managed anything. I replied that, indeed, I had managed a team, with two different levels below me, and a budget. Moreover, as a clinching statement I said, 'I have also actually sacked someone.' This helped persuade him that I had my feet on the ground.

I was always rated as a good manager by most subordinates and all my bosses. However, I concluded that this was not an area of great satisfaction for me. My real pleasure was in the things I did myself, rather than the things I got others to do. But the experience of being a manager is centrally relevant to my ability to help other managers. It is not just a question of having to face the ultimate decision of sacking someone. It is the fact of sitting with a variety of problems requiring decisions, often involving conflicting objectives. It is the experience of not being able to work on my priorities because subordinates, colleagues and clients want me to work on their problems. It is the experience of being able to say no to someone which enables me to suggest often, to managers with whom I now work as a consultant, that one of the best things they can do is to say no—to manage their own time and not let it be managed by others.

Feelings about People

I rarely have strong feelings about the people I interview, because I am reluctant to make my mind up quickly in the space of a couple of hours. This is also true of people I work with more intensively—even Sid, the director in case 2 who had many dislikeable characteristics, had some which I admired. I have worked successfully with an explosive chief executive I called 'the carpet chewer' and with a director who used to send me into giggles by asking to see me at '4.17 p.m.'.

Very occasionally I have strong negative feelings, sometimes about manner but more often about intelligence. I have met a few individuals who resemble President Eisenhower's comments on Senator Knowland: 'He proves there is no final answer to the question, "How stupid can you get?" '. I have met more people whose intellect and behaviour I admire, for example Colin in case 1. I certainly have no arrogant belief that I could do better than most of the managers I work with.

In terms of national culture, my experience is substantially dominated by people from the United Kingdom. There are of course significant differences here, so my experience in working with people in Scotland is not the same as that with people in St Helens or in London, and in the case of the first two there are regional characteristics that marginally affected some aspects of the way in which I work. I have worked with people from the United States, both here and there; I have worked in Australia; I have worked in South Africa, most excitingly but also most frustratingly (because of their different view about timekeeping) with emerging black African managers.

Until very recently, my experience was almost entirely with white male managers and directors: the cases here represent unfortunately the absence of other types at senior levels in most British organizations. A month before writing this chapter, I worked for the first time with a group of directors half of whom were women.

The Importance of Writing

In 1967, a journalist at a party asked whether I ever reviewed management books. At that time, the only review I had ever written was for the *Cambridge Labour* magazine in which I reviewed Anthony Crosland's *The Future of Socialism*. But I thought it was an interesting idea, so I reviewed a book for him. That led to my first article, and in 1971 I published my first book, *The Manager and Training*. I had never thought of writing a book, but an IPM Committee I then chaired was asked to recommend an author and chose to name me.

The next book, *Making Experience Pay* (McGraw-Hill, 1980), began to capture some of the themes that have been the basis of my continued work. I had been vaguely thinking about writing such a book for several years and had been collecting material, but the invitation to write it arrived as a handwritten postscript to a letter on a different subject from McGraw-Hill.

My first really 'planned' writing came from director research and was first published as a report 'Developing Directors: The Learning Processes', and was then extended as the core of my only research-based book, *Developing Top Managers* (Gower, 1988).

Management Development: Strategies for Action (IPM, 1993) also had a partially accidental origin. Several individuals over the years had said that I should write 'the' management development textbook, and I had pompously said that I had more important things to write. The coincidence of an accidental conversation at the Institute of Personnel Management and a considerable amount of material that I had not used in *Developing Top Managers* led me to write the book.

How Managers Can Develop Managers (Gower, 1993) was the first book I wrote without any external prompting. It actually came about from some dissatisfaction I had had with a major report called 'Developing the Developers', and a subsequent conference on 'The Line Managers as Developer'.

This current book returns to the previous pattern of responding to an external stimulus. Mike Pedler asked whether I would be interested in writing a book on my director-level experiences. This reactivated a half-buried series of notes I had made, not about running director programmes, but about a process of reflecting on the experience of running director programmes. This was an idea that David Boud mentioned to me on a trip to Australia.

Collaborative Writing

I get great satisfaction from writing. The material I have written with Peter Honey has given extra dimensions: first, the successful achievement of merging ourselves and our ideas; second, the transition from an agreeable work partnership to a deeply valued friendship. Although I initiated the work that led to our learning styles material, it was Peter's idea to publish it. Our other materials were all jointly identified and planned.

Learning from Writing

At this point, readers may be saying to themselves that this is all fascinating anecdotal information, but what does it really have to do with the theme of this book? There are two justifications for this review. First, I have understood better what I have actually experienced and learned as a result of writing books. However, that simple sentence conceals the fact that that until relatively recently I had not really understood the point. I had written books because I had such a strong desire to communicate. (The fact that I have received favourable reviews has helped to keep me writing—though I remember the two unfavourable ones clearly.) Recognition that writing the book did more than communicate, in that it forced me to go through the learning cycle more effectively than I otherwise had done came to me only with *How Managers Can Develop Managers* (Gower, 1993).

The second reason why this review of the origins of book writing is significant for organizational learning is that it is an example of an only partially recognized opportunity to learn from undertaking a task—a personal version of one of the themes of this book.

I have several times referred to the fact that I am a great user of irony and a collector of paradoxes, particularly in relation to my own experiences. The paradox of my relatively recent recognition that writing books is a structured form of learning for me is made even sharper by the fact that I have provided quite a lot of guidance about how other people should improve their learning by writing. My business school has three major features of its MBA programme which require learning through written reviews. I wrote the guidance on how to write a learning log, on how to complete the overall review which we call the 'Evaluative Assessment of Managerial Learning', and, something not mentioned in this book so far, on our Five-Year Continuing Renewal process: our graduands and faculty are asked to complete a review every five years of what they have learned, how they have learned it and what they will do now. We believe this to be a unique phenomenon, unfortunately taken up by a tiny minority. However, the good news is that it is vastly appreciated by those who actually do undertake it.

All this guidance I have written for others. I did a review of my experiences for my doctorate, I have done the five-year review myself and have learned from both. Yet I did not fully recognize my books as being a response in a different part of my working life to the same phenomenon of learning from review and writing. I have been a victim of the same seduction of task as compared with process which I have so often mentioned to other people as a constraint on effective learning.

**Understanding
What I Offer**

I am delighted when people tell me that in my work and in my writing I am seen as professional, practical, relevant. I think the ethos and practices of at least British business schools was for a long time dominated, and for many still is, by an approach to management education which is not only academic but fundamentally misplaced. Many business schools have tried to make management into an intellectual activity, because that is what people in business schools believe they understand and can offer. (Though they encourage Karaoke learning—you sing to their tune and words.) My profound belief is that management is an intelligent, not an intellectual, activity.

That is partly explained by the fact that I am not an intellectual, though I am certainly, as the tests show, intelligent on those dimensions that tests measure. Tony Benn, the left-wing British Labour MP, reversed the normal social process by becoming more of a socialist as he got older. When first elected as an MP, he made a public announcement that he must lose the stigma of being an intellectual. Anthony Crosland, his teacher at Oxford, and himself a major socialist thinker said 'You'd better acquire the stigma before worrying about losing it.'

I struggle with other people's theories, let alone with attempting to produce my own. I have explicitly to set myself a task of producing models because otherwise I would not do so. I was surprised to find from reading B. Holmberg's *The Theory and Practice of Distance Education* (Routledge, 1989) that the style I have used in this book is 'guided didactic conversation'. This means that it is conversational, informal and uses my own experience. Holmberg's description represents the intellectual's complication of communication which removes it from the comprehension of many managers. I avoid using words I have to explain to managers, especially if there is an alternative (all right, synonym). So I avoid:

• Andragogy (except when I want to tease academics)
• Holistic
• Paradigm
• Deuterolearning

18   Contributions to a Learning Organization

In this book contributions of different kinds in different organizations have been tested against the definition of a learning organization produced by Peter Honey and myself (see page xx).

Personal Learning

This is a book about how I have facilitated the learning of others; but it is also a much more personal record of my own learning about the issues and practices involved in facilitating others.

Learning is a search for meaning. Among the important meanings for me are:

1. Experience is always at the core of learning. New experiences provide skills, knowledge and insight; but they are tested against learning derived from earlier experiences. Skills, knowledge and insight derived from formal inputs, not usually seen as 'experiences' in the same sense, in fact become meaningful by being tested against existing knowledge, skills and insights. A major feature of this book has been that the conscious, deliberate and effective integration of learning from real work and learning through structured inputs is likely to be the most effective process for most managers, most of the time.
2. Learning is essentially an individual and a personal experience. It is individual because we differ one from another in our needs and wants in terms of development. It is personal because learning draws upon tests and responds to deeper aspects of our values, beliefs and behaviours. What I have described as 'individual' is to a significant extent responsive to analytical and diagnostic intervention. The 'personal' aspects are less responsive to analysis and diagnosis, and even more subject to problems in defining and sustaining effective action.

In many ways the book represents this dichotomy. It has been deliberately designed and implemented in terms of what I as an individual can describe and assess. It has also attempted to bring in more of the personal factors that have been at play while I have been carrying out the work described here.

Continuing the Individual and Personal Theme

My last two books (*Management Development: Strategies for Action*, IPM, 2nd ed, 1993 and *How Managers Can Develop Managers*, Gower, 1993) not only describe desirable actions, but also provide a series of exercises to be undertaken by readers to test their own understanding, and their own preferred actions. In contrast, this book provides no exercises for the reader. It is centred on a series of experiences, and on my conclusions about those experiences, in relation to which it is reasonable to assume that most readers will be testing their own beliefs and values and experiences. This approach was deliberately chosen as an encouragement to myself to keep the book personal and close to my own experiences, without pressing readers to do the same. Exercises might have provided a more distancing effect than I wanted.

A second reason actually challenges some of the philosophy behind my normal approach—a challenge that is particularly appropriate for this book. Exercises are in a significant sense a statement from me to the reader about what the reader should find valuable and should do about whatever it is I have been describing in the book. I know this is a good, because very practical, feature for a lot of readers. I was, however, struck recently, when reading a book on facilitation skills, of a potential problem engendered by this approach. The book attempted to describe the author's criticisms of many training courses as being designed and implemented too much in accordance with the trainer's interests, and not sufficiently with the real experiences and concerns of people attending courses. It seemed to me unfortunate, not to say contradictory, that the authors then set out at the beginning of each chapter the learning outcomes they intended the readers to secure from reading the chapter.

So for this book, while offering strong views about why I have done what I have done, I have done less than I normally do in suggesting what readers should do about what I have done.

The Environment for Learning

The learning pyramid (Fig. 18.1) is changed from the learning hierarchy shown in Chapter 9. I now introduce the concept

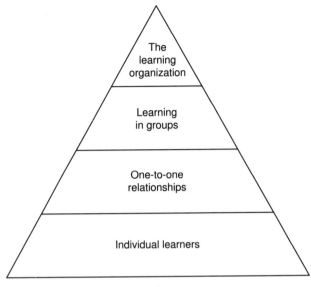

Learning becomes qualitatively and quantitatively
more difficult as you ascend the pyramid

Figure 18.1   The learning pyramid

that the level of learning needs to be understood also in terms of quantity and likelihood.

The base of the pyramid, the individual, is where all learning has to start, where it is most likely to occur, and where therefore, if one were able to assess the amount of learning, most learning will have been achieved.

The next level, one-to-one relationships, represents a major feature for most learners, often not fully recognized, used or achieved. Even in principle it is likely to contain less learning than the individual level, simply because of the additional complications involved in one-to-one relationships.

The third level, learning within groups, is similarly limited in terms of recognition and achievement, and even more complicated than one-to-one relationships in terms of the likely problems of interaction between members of the group.

Finally, we reach the top of the pyramid, the learning organization as a total achievement. This is the peak in terms of significance, but the smallest in terms of quantity and likelihood. The metaphor involved, representing the fact that you have to climb up the pyramid and that it gets more difficult as you proceed towards the top, seems most appropriate.

Some of my work, especially the personal development

plans, has been focused primarily on individual learners. Some of it has brought in both individual and group learning (see especially cases 4, 5 and 7). Some of it has provided opportunities for one-to-one helping relationships (case 5 in some measure, case 7 as an explicit purpose). None of the cases have responded to an explicit or implicit objective of creating a learning organization.

In addition to the points just made about the levels at which my intervention operated in terms of learning relationships, there is an interesting issue about the organizational levels involved. Most of the cases quoted here involve two levels: predominantly board level and below board level. Sometimes the levels were explicitly a feature of a single project; sometimes they were involved through different projects. Case 2 involved work at three levels, but through two different projects. Case 5 involved managers and directors but in two different programmes, the middle-management programme being one of the stimuli for the director development programme.

The conclusion I have come to on this point is that in future work I should:

1. Provide more explicit encouragement to the client to think in terms of the learning pyramid. Despite the attractiveness of the term 'learning organization' to many management development advisers and personnel directors, I will be using the learning pyramid as a better and more practical theme than the learning organization alone.
2. Give even more encouragement than I have already done to the development of effective interaction between the different levels in the pyramid.
3. Give a special emphasis on developing more effective one-to-one relationships, because these constitute the reality of managerial life, because the responsibilities involved are relatively clear, and because the behaviours and practices to be encouraged can be defined and practised.
4. Make more explicit offers to management development specialists within organizations to enable them to carry out implementation of ideas about the learning pyramid.

Behaviours and Practices

As discussed in the previous chapter, there is some conflict between my relatively high score on abstract conceptualization in the Kolb Learning Styles Inventory, and my Moderate Theorist score on my own Learning Styles Questionnaire. I suspect that my approach to and beliefs about the learning organization reflect the latter. The idea of a learning organization as a conceptual goal does not turn me on; more important, I suspect that many managers will not be turned on by a pure concept—unless of course they are Strong Theorists.

So the emphasis in my work is about the development of behaviours and practices.

It is interesting to note that Peter Senge, who has done so much to place the learning organization on the agenda, has done so in the context of, and with the perspective of, organizations as systems. I value his work, while taking a different view about what kind of system we should be looking at for organizational learning. One part of the system is clearly the formal management development processes—appraisal, resource plans, personal development plans. These formal systems are tremendously important. However, as I have already suggested in *Management Development: Strategies for Action* (IPM, 2nd ed, 1993), I think that a lot of the energy devoted to these existing formal processes could well be shifted into the areas discussed in this book.

Specifically, my work will continue to focus on developing systems for learning in and around the work done by managers and directors. In order to achieve this, I will continue to encourage the development of a systematic approach to learning by individuals and groups. In addition, I will be giving greater emphasis to the idea of discipline. My use of that word is, again, rather different from that of Senge, but it contains the same principle: learning must be picked up as systematic, regular, disciplined in the managerial sense. The kind of discipline I would encourage means that managers will continually assess their own performance as learners, and will ensure that colleagues and groups with whom they are involved similarly discuss their achievements and difficulties and failures in terms of learning.

The Task, Learning and Individuality

A systematic and disciplined set of behaviours and practices will continue to involve recognizing tasks and learning experiences. The task cycle and learning cycle can be introduced side by side as in Fig. 18. 2.

I have experimented with merging the two cycles. This can be done by drawing the task cycle around the learning cycle, or the learning cycle around the task cycle—see Fig. 18.3.

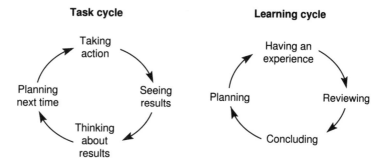

Figure 18.2   Separate task and learning cycles
Source: P. Honey and A. Mumford, *Manual of Learning Opportunities*, Honey, 1989

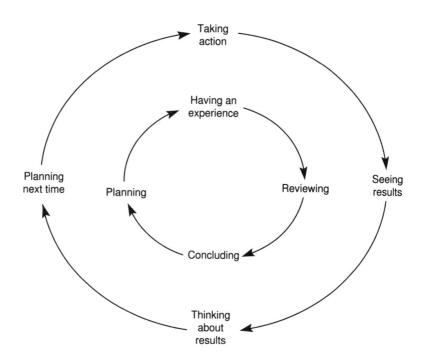

Figure 18.3   Combined task and learning cycles
Source: P. Honey and A. Mumford, *Manual of Learning Opportunities*, Honey, 1989

There are arguments for either of these figures. I used to favour the learning cycle being drawn around the task cycle, because it was in a sense added on. I now present the learning cycle inside the task cycle, because I think that for many managers the idea of learning being contained within the task, rather than superimposed, has some advantage. Even more important, perhaps, this enables me to say that I recognize that the task is actually much the most important element in real-world learning, but quantitively learning, is an element within the task.

The third element then is to build in the learning styles issue, which demonstrates the crucial relationship between the general discipline that individuals or groups can adopt to improve their learning and the individual element, which shows how interested they are likely to be at particular stages of the cycle. The recognition of individual strengths and relative weaknesses is crucial not only for each individual, but also in the one-to-one relationships and in groups where, of course, the potential for drawing on each other's strengths offers so much.

Continuous Learning   The interaction between task and learning described throughout this book is the prerequisite for continuous learning and development. Learning focused in and through work can be continuous, but it can be improved through the disciplined behaviours and practices outlined above. Focus on real work removes the exaggerated attention to one-off courses. I have gone part-way in not just encouraging the interaction between task and learning, but providing for greater continuity through the programmes described here. I need to do more, particularly in the area of learning reviews during programmes, developing effective interactions, and substantial disciplined reviews of programmes after they have been completed.

Personal development plans, learning agreements and the whole process of self-development provide a clearer path for continuous learning. Again, the problem for the outsider is to follow up with the clients on what has actually happened; this requires a relatively brave statement from me to clients that they ought to engage me to do this.

Incremental more than Transformational Learning   My current definition of learning is:

People can demonstrate that they know something that they did not know before (insights and realizations) and/or when they do something they could not do before (skills). (Peter Honey and Alan Mumford, *Manual of Learning Styles*, Honey, 3rd ed, 1992).

I expect to continue to work mainly at levels of incremental rather than transformational learning. This is partly a matter of what my clients are likely to continue to want. It is partly also what I have a predisposition to believe, i.e. that transformational learning is extremely difficult. Again, my occasional sense of modesty affects this, in the sense that I recognize that I am better at building from current realities than at offering transformation. Moreover, the practical point is likely to continue to be that, if the people I work with have not fully understood how they have learned to deal with their current realities, and what they need to learn to deal with them better, the likelihood of their achieving successful transformational learning is not very high.

Should this seem too cautious and limited a view, it is worth saying that many of the people I have been involved with would talk about major and significant changes in their learning, their managerial practices and their effectiveness. Perhaps the question is largely semantic—at what level of change does learning become transformational?

Entry Points

The entry point for the work described here has been analytic and diagnostic. All has revolved around questions about what the issues were for the organizations with which I was going to be involved, the reality of the problems and opportunities they faced. I am clear that that is the approach I will continue to suggest. I am good at it, I enjoy doing it, and it provides a much more effective base for work which managers themselves recognize as being relevant. In terms of my model most are type 3 management development (page 106).

However, once the process is under way, and particularly once we get involved in discussions about learning, emphasis on formal analytical and diagnostic approaches can be balanced with informal opportunistic processes. A major part of the learning opportunities available for individuals occur without being planned, and the learning that may be derived from them occurs without being planned either. One part of my work is to enable people to recognize more clearly in advance what kind of opportunities exist or can be created and how they can learn from them. But a major part of my efforts will continue to be to enable managers to learn from opportunities that they have not planned or recognized in advance; to persuade them (through a type 3 process) to convert type 1 into type 2. The learning organization recognizes and uses all three types. The large number of managers who do not use the Prospective approach, and cannot be encouraged to do so, must be helped at least to gain benefit from hindsight, reviewing of unplanned opportunities. My endeavours here will be to help individuals, pairs and groups to adopt learning reviews as a regular discipline.

Recognizing and using learning opportunities at least in retrospect is the practical focus for many of us. The workbook that Peter Honey and I wrote on this (*The Opportunist Learner* Honey, 2nd ed, 1995) looks at both formal and informal ways of recognizing and using learning opportunities, and defines the opportunist learner as one who:

- Looks for a wide variety of opportunities for learning
- Continuously develops knowledge, skills and insights
- Manages learning—by setting objectives and measuring achievements
- Has short-term learning targets and often longer-term goals as well
- Uses a variety of resources for learning, i.e. job experiences, courses, distance learning, reading, experiences outside work, colleagues and professional helpers
- Understands and makes use of principles of effective learning, especially in developing personal learning skills.

'Opportunist' is a word that carries some negative vibrations. I will happily continue to work with managers to explain the term. They are always delighted to know that I do not mean a person who sacrifices principle, but rather, someone who responds creatively to chances, challenges, problems—to all of these as learning opportunities.

One More Time   I will continue to undertake learning reviews on specific programmes and on work with clients. I will continue to carry out a review every two months of what I have done and what I have learned—having learned from a previous learning review how much I was missing by not doing it so regularly! I will continue these things because I know that:

- I will benefit in terms of personal understanding and satisfaction.
- My clients will benefit because my work will continue to develop and improve.
- I will be able to answer positively those managers who ask me if I keep learning logs and do learning reviews as I advocate on my programmes.

INDEX